THE HURDLES AND PITFALLS OF REAL ESTATE INVESTING

by

Russell A. Whitney

Whitney Leadership Group, Inc.
1612 East Cape Coral Pkwy
Cape Coral, FL 33904

1st Publicaton as "Overcoming the Hurdles and Pitfalls of Real Estate Investing," 1984
Reprinted 1985, 1986, 1987, 1988, 1989, 1990, 1991
Revised as "The Hurdles and Pitfalls of Real Estate Investing," 1992

This book is designed to provide accurate and authoritative information with regard to the subject matter covered. It is sold with the understanding that the author and publisher are not engaged in rendering legal or accounting services. If legal advice or other expert assistance is required, the services of a competent professional person should be sought. (From a Declaration of Principles jointly adopted by a committee of the American Bar Association and a Committee of Publishers and Associations).

Acknowledgments

This book has been long in the making. It would be impossible for me to thank all of the people who have helped me to achieve the things about which you will read.

I owe a special debt of gratitude to my family, for their support and unwavering faith through the lean years.

To Ingrid, my wife of sixteen years, who has worked endlessly to keep the books and records, care for the children and be patient with my whims.

To the late Russell Walter Whitney (1931-1970), my father, my foundation. I only wish you could be here today.

To my son, the new Russell W. Whitney.

To Thea, the Goddess of Love, my daughter.

To you, the reader, for having the strength to seek a more fulfilling life-one of adventure and achievement.

Last, but not least, to the vast majority. To all of those who said it could not be done. You gave me the inspiration to prove you wrong. Thank you.

Preface-1992

It's been several years since the first publication of this book detailing my early real estate transactions. Some of the greatest rewards I've had, since then, have been from the many people who have sent me letters. They all have said, in essence: "Your book is so easy to read and follow. It gives such a good foundation, it almost makes me feel like you're right here, showing me step-by-step exactly how to do it."

I wrote *The Hurdles and Pitfalls Of Real Estate Investing*, initially, to share the real story of my experiences, as well as the trials and tribulations of getting started. From the beginning, I was determined to tell people the things that other books didn't. For these reasons, I have not wanted to change any of the actual content of the book, just to update the philosophies and preface each new printing.

As my best (or worst) critic, I review this book regularly. At times, I have thought the book dated, whenever the real estate market experienced drastic change or interest rates fluctuated markedly. But it really wasn't, and isn't dated today, as long as you understand there are cycles of change in real estate, like everything else.

When I first started investing, interest rates were around 8%. Later, they had fallen as low as 4%, and I remember commenting, "Look how much better the real estate market is because interest rates have come down." Once, when we hit a recession for a while, it got even easier to buy property than when I first started.

To put all this in perspective...I think you will agree, real estate is more expensive, now, than it was fifteen years ago...or twenty-five years ago...even <u>two hundred</u> years ago. You must constantly ask yourself, "Will real estate be more expensive ten years from now?" The answer is always yes!

So the fundamentals of this book <u>haven't</u> changed. Of course, there will always be new techniques to learn. My follow-up and future books will continue to detail new breakthroughs

For now, I hope you enjoy reading the story of the hurdles and pitfalls of my early years, and how I believe, you, too, can make a million in Real Estate.

Foreword
from the first edition, 1984

There are several reasons why I have written this book. Before I explain, let me say that I have put this writing off time and again for the past four years. My reasoning probably could be attributed to the fact that I had many goals to achieve for myself, first.

As you read on, I am sure you will understand my motivation. I had just celebrated my 27th birthday. During the previous four and a half years I had purchased over $4,000,000 worth of income producing property. I lived comfortably, but had not reached the magnitude of success the many "How to Make A Million" authors claimed they had. I personally believed there was quite a lot of exaggeration in most of their books.

Many reveal methods of achieving wealth, raising capital, locating super buys and so forth. What they don't tell you is how successful people continue to grow, step by step. They don't tell you what to do when the bank refuses to lend you money, or when you run across obstacles that stop you dead. Nor do they tell you how to stay "on track."

When you have applied what you've read, followed the techniques to the letter, and have seriously given it an honest try...why doesn't it work? What are you doing wrong? You put in many offers but are not finding any so-called, "no money down deals."

Your mind begins to echo, "When I ask someone to sell a property for *no money down,* they look at me like I have two heads!" You resort to, "It may have worked for them, but the economy was different. Anybody could get a loan then. How hard could it be to get a positive cash flow when interest rates are 8-1/2%?"

I didn't graduate from high school or attend a formal college. In pursuit of education, I have read hundreds of "how to" books on almost every subject. When I read my first book on achieving riches through income properties, I was working in a slaughterhouse, killing hogs for $5.00 an hour.

Reading that one book started me on the road to using realistic techniques for achieving financial independence through income property investing. One year later, I had accumulated several hundred thousand dollars worth of property. Then, all of a sudden, the market changed. Banks tightened their lending policies, and I couldn't find any "no money down deals." Sellers didn't offer the deals anymore, and I found myself floundering and failing terribly.

I lost almost two years of growth toward my goals. I was virtually unable to find a deal, make an investment, or get a loan. Then, one day, after months of research, I discovered some very important solutions to my problems.

What I discovered helped me understand why things weren't working for me anymore. I found out why average people, just like you and me, weren't making the big money the "experts'" books say we should. It astounded me how uncomplicated the answers really were. From that day on, I turned my life around... and so can you!

The following is a detailed account of what happened from the first day I read the book on investing in income property. I narrate negotiations with each seller and banker. By using these same techniques, you can accomplish your goals and discover exactly what your capabilities truly are.

In the pages that follow, you will learn, first hand, my personal secrets that will make the difference between failure and success. The following is a documented fact I will explain to you, in detail: Three weeks following my discovery, I purchased five separate properties totaling 21 units and valued at about half a million dollars, with absolutely no money of my own! These properties had a positive cash flow of $22,000 a year. I also made approximately $25,000 shortly after the closings by pulling out equity. And I made still another $18,000 several weeks after. I explain exactly how to do just what I did in this book.

If you have read other books on the path to personal wealth, this book is a must for you! It is written in easy to read language, and is accurate within pennies. I have not added fluff or exaggeration, just hard facts. If, after finishing the book, you don't feel you can surpass your present economic position, don't waste anymore money on real estate investing books.

It's not for you!

Table of Contents

Chapter One

How I Got Started At The Age of 20

My story begins in March, 1976. I lived in Schenectady, a small town in upstate New York, just west of Albany. I applied and was hired for the best job I'd ever had, at the Tobin Packing Company, Inc. I was a laborer on a production line in the slaughterhouse. My responsibilities were to shackle 1,400 doomed hogs a day before they were killed. The pay was $5 an hour, and with overtime, I was making over $300 a week. Iwas 20 years old, and I thought that this was the greatest job in the world. I had every intention of staying there for the next 30 years until I retired on a pension.

It took me about one year to decide that I was too smart to do that for the rest of my life and needed to find something more challenging. Since I was married and my wife was pregnant with our first child, I couldn't quit unless I had something definite to go to.

Hating this job more and more every day, and not wanting just another time card to punch, I started reading all of the "get rich quick" schemes advertised in the back of magazines and newspapers. I'm sure most of my readers can identify with the ads I'm talking about—"Lazy Man's Way to Wealth," "Mail Order Millions Over-Nite," "Send one letter and make $300,000 per year for the rest of your life," etc., etc.

Needless to say, I was getting discouraged. I had almost resigned myself to the slaughterhouse when I read a full page newspaper ad offering a book on investing in real estate. The ad attracted me for two reasons: 1) It offered a money back guarantee (note: I had spent hundreds of dollars on money-making ads with no results), and, 2) it didn't promise riches overnight. It seemed to require time and effort to make it happen. It made so much sense that I approached my wife on investing another $10 in our future. After selling her on another "get rich quick" deal, off went the check.

About three to four weeks and 20,000 hogs later, it came. I was always excited when I received new literature, hoping it would finally be the key to unlock my capabilities.

I opened the package and started reading the book. That was about 3:00 p.m. Even after my wife had fixed dinner and gone to bed, I was still reading. I could not put that book down. I finally finished it at 4:00 a.m. the next morning. I was so excited that I couldn't sit still. I woke my wife up and carried on for awhile about getting rich and buying all these properties, before I realized she had no idea what I was talking about. After explaining it a little more slowly and having her read some of the book, I started plotting my course of action.

Everything clicked. It made a tremendous amount of sense. N*ot* a "get rich quick scheme," but a steady, methodical, simple way to financial freedom. Note that I said *simple,* not easy. I knew that my educational background had not peaked with a GED diploma. I had the intelligence and motivation to achieve something big in my life. I only lacked the knowledge; someone to show me just once how it was done.

But let me get back to my story. My wife and I had purchased an old house several months before. It was uninhabitable when we bought it. There was no back door, and no kitchen facilities other than an old tub sink. The bathroom was out on the back porch. We purchased the house for $18,000, with $4,000 of our hard-earned money as a down payment. The owner held the mortgage of $14,000 for 15 years at 8-1/2 percent. Our payment was $142 per month. The month before we moved in, we used $1,500 and fixed up the kitchen. With my brother-in-law's help, we installed a new floor, walls, cabinets, a ceiling, and a back door. Keep in mind, I knew nothing about hanging sheet rock or remodeling. I asked many questions and just learned as I went along. Finally, we moved into the house in March, 1977. I was 21 years old. Over the next several months, we improved the house a little at a time. After staying up all night reading the book, it hit me like a ton of bricks. I was already on the right track without even knowing it.

How Did I Begin with No Money?

The first thing I did was to go to my bank and refinance the house. I told them I wanted to install aluminum siding, at a cost of $4,000.

Since I owed only $14,000 on the house, and, with all our improvements, the house was now worth $25,000-$30,000, I was confident that they would lend me the money. Well, the bank came out to appraise the house and said they would lend $18,000, but they wanted a first mortgage, indicating that I would have to pay off the existing one first. My brain still clicking, I called the man from whom I bought the house. I told him I had really done a super job improving it and I was planning to put some aluminum siding on. Before I explained my plan to him, I asked him to come and look at the house. My next move was to tell him, ever so innocently, that the bank would lend me the money to do the work, but they wanted a first mortgage position. I told him I would give him $7,000 right away if he would hold the other $7,000 I owed him in a second mortgage for 20 years at 8-1/2 %. He agreed, since it would be a safe move due to the condition of the house. At the closing, the bank gave me $18,000. We immediately closed on the second mortgage and I gave him $7,000 of the $18,000. I was only 21, and my wife and I were off to the bank to deposit $9,500. We were in shock for days. We absolutely could not believe how easy it had been! (I'll explain later why it was $9,500 instead of $11,000.)

Now, between the time I arranged the new mortgages and actually closed, I called a multitude of Realtors, as the "how to" book directed, until I ran across a unique agent. Thank you, Gary Sanders, of Schenectady, New York. I told him all about the book I had read and how I had all this money to buy any income property he could find. I also laid down the tough parameters of purchase. Gary was new to the real estate business and was as excited as I was. We met and talked for hours. Within several days we had presented many offers on two-family houses in the most distressed area of town. I was relatively new to Schenectady and didn't even know how to get to these places. Finally, we had an offer accepted on the worst looking house on Hulett Street. The asking price was $10,000. The offer was accepted at $6,500 cash. In my excitement, I went to the bank again and asked them to lend me the whole $6,500, since I had bought at such a steal. I laugh now, but I was so young and green, so unsophisticated about banking procedures that I didn't realize things just weren't done this way. When they explained this to me, I went home and got the book and marched right back to the bank to show them. I told them it could be done—it said so right here! I didn't understand why they needed several loan officers there, either; but because of my persistence, they agreed to lend me $5,000 for a first mortgage and deduct $1,500 from the proceeds of the $18,000 mortgage on my house as the down payment on the two-family house on Hulett Street. So, we actually had three closings from that first transaction in June, 1978!

The monthly payment on the $18,000 was $159. The second mortgage to the owner ($7,000) on my house was $69 per month. The $5,000 mortgage on the two-family house was $62 per month. Our payments on all the mortgages totaled $290 per month. We covered all the payments with the rent from the two-family house and still had $9,500 in the bank. I will not forget the empathy and assistance of the loan officer at the trust company. Thank you for all of your help.

My wife and I went to work on the two-family. We painted the outside, paneled the hallways, did some landscaping, and raised the rents to $185 for each flat. My daughter was now 10 months old and my wife and I still maintained our full time jobs. I remember many days (I worked nights and my wife, days) when I would take my daughter to the property and put her in the playpen outside while I was up 30 feet on the ladder, painting.

In the interim, between working full time and fixing the properties, I was still submitting offers with Gary Sanders, my friend and Realtor.

Nothing happened from June until November of 1978, almost five months. Gary was negotiating on a five-unit brick building at 11 Eagle Street that listed for $44,000. Our offers were in the range of $32,000 with $3,000 down. We were to assume the first mortgage and have the owner hold a second mortgage for the balance.

This purchase had to be drawn in the form of a land contract (contract for deed[1]) since the first mortgage was not assumable. We finally settled at a purchase price of $37,000 with $4,000 down. By deducting the prorated rents[2], we closed on the five-unit for only $2,850 actual out of pocket. Our net rents after mortgage, taxes, insurance and utilities were about $2,340 per year. That was almost 100% return in the first year just on the cash! We still had $6,650 left from our original $9,500.

As the saying goes, when it rains it pours. Gary had been working on the purchase of two four-unit buildings located on the same street as the five-unit. The owner had moved to Florida and the buildings were really in disrepair. They were mismanaged and had many vacancies. We negotiated the purchase of both four-unit buildings

(23-25 and 21 Eagle St.) for a total of $5,000 down and a $50,000 sale price. Actually, we paid $2,500 down for each one. After the prorated rents, our out of pocket monies totaled $3,500 for both buildings. These closings took place rather quickly; the two-family in June, the five-unit on December 3rd, and the very next month, on January 3, the two four-units.

We were now up to a total of sixteen units, with a rent roll of $34,000 per year and a decent net cash flow. I was growing very impatient at the slaughterhouse. I dreaded going to work in the morning, but I knew it was just a matter of time before the rents would support us.

I was still following the "how to" book to the letter. I also supplemented my reading with monthly real estate newsletters and virtually every book I could buy or borrow pertaining to real estate.

I was constantly looking for more property and Gary was presenting offers on a regular basis. The book's advice about finding a good, hungry Realtor played a major part in our early success.

Gary was learning a lot about real estate investing and we discussed going into a partnership on some purchases. About one month after we closed the two four-units, Gary found a deal on two three-unit buildings right next to each other.

The lady who owned them was 65 years old. Her husband had died and she was unable to manage or maintain them. They were run down, the tenants were not paying the rent, and she wanted out. The properties were in a marginal area which helped us negotiate exceptional terms. The two properties, 335 and 337 Hulett Street, were on the other end of the street from where I had made my first purchase of the two family, 455 Hulett Street.

We finally settled on $7,500 as a purchase price for each property, a total of $15,000 with $2,000 down and the seller holding the $13,000 mortgage. After the prorated rents, Gary and I each came out of pocket with $800 for the closing. Our mortgage payment was $130 per month, which covered both properties, and the rent roll was $990 per month.

So far, so good, but it got even better. The properties needed quite a bit of fixing up. At this time in New York, the banks were giving FHA Title I Home Improvement Loans[3]. Equity had nothing to do with qualifying. All that was needed was a contractor's estimate for the improvements and a reasonable credit rating.

I provided the estimate on my own letterhead for $15,000. We applied for the loan and three weeks later received a check for that amount. Gary and I did most of the work, and upon completion it had only cost $5,000. We compensated ourselves with $5,000 apiece for two weeks of labor. We had added a fourth unit to 335 Hulett, thus giving us seven units instead of six. By the way, not only did we increase the cash flow by increasing rents, but we didn't have to pay taxes on the $5,000 we paid ourselves, since it came out of loan money, which of course is non-taxable as ordinary income. The $15,000 home improvement loan at 12% for 12 years cost $197 per month, which was easily covered by the rents and still left us a handsome profit. I eventually sold my half of the investment to Gary for $1,000. He then sold it for $1,000 with the buyer assuming the mortgage and the home improvement loan. This was one of the most profitable investments (in percentages) I've ever made. I was now up to 23 units and still hungry, at 23 years of age, to achieve financial freedom.

[1] See appendix. [2] See appendix. [3] See appendix.

Should I Quit My Job?

Between January and March of 1979, I took the test for my real estate license and passed. Gary had made quite a bit of money in commissions on my purchases and I figured that having my license would give me insight into the good deals before they hit the market. I was doing most of my own work on finding deals now and I was writing the offers myself and just giving them to Gary to present. I also thought I could make enough in commissions to enable me to quit my job at the slaughterhouse. Now came the big decision. My wife and I discussed it and the decision was made on March 1979. I was free! I felt like the weight of the whole world was lifted from my shoulders on that day. I'll never forget it. My wife's parents were in shock. My fellow employees, friends, and union officers thought I was crazy. My wife's father had worked there for 22 years. He had been a good provider for his family. There I had job security, a pension, and the best benefits around. People waited for years to get into the Tobin Packing Company. They were the highest paying meat packing house in the country. The union officers tried to talk me out of quitting. I had seniority time built up and a vacation coming.

"Russ, think about your future," they said. "Think about your family." "I am thinking of them," I said. "Thank you for your concern. I quit!"

There was enough cash flow from all of our properties to pay our bills and put gas in the cars, with some to spare. I had it all figured out before we made the decision.

You wouldn't believe how many people, relatives included, told me I could never do what I've done. I've kept several phrases in front of me where I can see them every day. I hope you remember these ever so important words:

"For as a man thinketh in his own heart, so is he."

"For every one person who says you can do it, twenty will say you can't."

Several weeks before I quit my job, I applied again to the trust company for another FHA home improvement loan of $12,000. I needed more investment capital. The improvements were to be made on my house, the two-family, at 455 Hulett Street, and the five-unit, 11 Eagle Street.

The loan was approved. The net rents were more than sufficient to cover the $176 per month payment. Just to keep things straight, the first home improvement loan Gary and I took out was with a different bank. I used about $4,000 for the improvements and kept $8,000 for more investments. Also, since I no longer had my job, I was a little security conscious.

Let me summarize events up to this point before I continue.

It had been ten months since I read the "how to" book and made my first investment, in June of 1978. I now owned 23 units (seven buildings) with $45,000 per year gross rents. I had secured over $40,000 from refinancing my house and taking the home improvement loans. I also had another $5,000 open line of credit with Citibank. That is another amazing story. One day I received a letter in the mail from Citibank. Upon filling out the enclosed application, they said they would send me a checkbook which could be used at any time up to a $5,000 limit. I never even went to the bank or spoke with a loan officer! It had just been one phenomenal event after another since I started my career in real estate investing. Ten months, 23 units and $45,000 later, I had $15,000 in the bank. I was just 23 years old.

I now had my real estate license and became associated with a

Realty company in Schenectady. I was very excited about this new freedom and told everyone that I was in the real estate business. I felt that I had a lot more experience than most of the associates in the office so I wasn't shy about getting started. Through one acquaintance and a phone call, I ended up with three listings and two sales in that first month. I made over $3,000 in commissions in four weeks! Comparing my last ten months' earnings and the progress I had made in the real estate field with the $14,000 a year I made at the slaughterhouse, I was totally convinced that I had made the right decision.

I was also very conscious of the fact that the real money is made by investing, and not through commissions. I kept looking for more properties.

Is There Such a Thing As A No Money Down Purchase?

An investor called me that month. He was the fellow who lived in Florida and had sold me the two four-unit buildings on Eagle Street in January. As it turned out, he also owned a six-unit building on Eagle Street. I had passed by it dozens of times and never knew he owned it. It caught my eye on several occasions, though, because it was the most deteriorated property on the block. It was badly in need of a paint job, and had many broken windows. A management company was handling it for him, and, obviously, they were doing a terrible job. He frequently came to New York on business and had seen the properties I had purchased from him. He liked the new paint on the four-unit building, as well as the shrubs and new storm windows and screens that I had put in with the home improvement money. Since he was, and still is, holding the mortgage on these properties, he knew that I would be an excellent prospect for him to sell the six-unit to. We negotiated on and off until April, 1979, without reaching a deal. I knew he was motivated, so I waited. I wanted a no money down purchase and he was hoping for a large down payment plus an excessive purchase price.

We finally settled on a partnership. Since there was no mortgage on the property, we agreed that he and I would buy the building and give a mortgage back to his wife for $25,000. That was also to be the purchase price, *with no money down.* After some cosmetic improvements, I placed the value at about $75,000. We also agreed to co-sign a note to the bank for another $15,000 home improvement loan. I must say, the HIL's were helpful and pretty easy to get.

My side of the partnership included management, maintenance and handling the renovations. We would split all profit and depreciation down the middle.

We closed almost immediately. Within three weeks, we had a $15,000 check for the improvements. This was my first major renovation. I gutted three apartments completely and put in new toilets, tubs, sinks, cabinets, sheet rock, and drop ceilings. I subcontracted the installation of a furnace and a new roof. It was too expensive to put aluminum siding on the whole building, so I just had the front done to dress it up, and painted the other three sides to match. The buildings on either side were pretty close together so it looked fine without incurring a major expense. A new front porch and steps were built, too.

I learned from the competitive bidding of all the various contractors. It was also very interesting trying to keep everyone working in sequence without getting in each others way. As the job progressed, I rented out the finished apartments and raised rents on the others.

Five weeks later, our $15,000 renovation had turned into about $19,000. Rather than use our own monies, I used rents and securities to cover some of the $4,000 overage. I also arranged payment plans with several of the contractors.

It looked beautiful when it was done. We had a 100% occupancy from the very first month, with a $15,600 annual rent roll.

We kept this property (16 Eagle Street) for about a year before we decided to dissolve the partnership and sell it. Guess who bought it? None other than my friend and Realtor, Gary Sanders. Gary had been accumulating some properties also. We made him a very good deal for $51,000. He assumed the $25,000 mortgage along with the $15,000 home improvement loan. He gave us $5,500 in a down payment and we held $5,500 in a third mortgage. The investor and I split like this: I took the $5,500 cash and he took the paper.

After 16 Eagle Street, I began to look at some bigger properties. The bank was treating me more cordially, too. My dealings were now with the main branch of the bank. I worked with the vice-president in charge of commercial mortgages and loans. I came to him recommended by the branch office, where I got my initial loan.

My First Roadblock—The Bank

The vice-president of the bank was a very, very conservative fellow. He could appear to be very unsophisticated, but he was as sharp as Colombo. As our relationship matured, he me very fairly. Initially, though, I had a very hard time getting him to take me seriously. In his eyes I was only a kid, yet I owned several hundred thousand dollars of property, had a healthy bank account and enough enthusiasm to make a room hum. You see, he was the man who had appraised my house for refinancing 10 months before. He knew my wife and I when we had less than $1,000 in the bank and one little, run-down house. He had seen the changes I had made in my life in just short ten months.

I had found several good properties containing seventeen or more units. The owner of one project in particular was being transferred out of town and was very motivated to sell. The price and terms were so unbelievably low, I thought there had to be something wrong with the building.

There were three or four vacancies and the property needed some interior painting, along with some other minor cosmetic improvements. After carefully inspecting this building, I was satisfied that I was getting an excellent deal. The owner was going to sell a 17-unit brick building for $70,000!

He didn't want to hold any paper, so I had to try to arrange financing. Except for my first deal back in June, I had not purchased anything with bank financing. Everything had been through owner financing.

I prepared a rent roll and expense sheet for the bank. The gross rents were about $36,000 per year with a net cash flow of approximately $17,000 after all expenses, including the mortgage. This would have been one heck of a purchase had the following problems not occurred. First of all, I had to get approval from the vice-president of the bank. Our relationship was still relatively new. He humored me and took my application for mortgage with the fee of $100. It is still my belief that he never had any intention of granting the loan. I think at this time he was trying to slow me down so that I didn't get in over my head. I also believe there was some genuine concern for me in several of his denials, as well as some jealousy. As I look back upon some of my requests, it is obvious to me that I might have made some bad decisions. The 17-unit was not one, and I believe that to this day. As you may have guessed, the bank denied the mortgage. I was so angry, like a spoiled kid I threatened to take my money and business elsewhere. I went to several other banks in an attempt to arrange financing on the building.

I finally concluded that the banks were redlining[4] this area. I also felt that they were discriminating against me because of my age. They felt that I was too young to be eligible for such a big loan. Whatever the reason, I didn't want to let them slow me down. I had goals to meet. I called my attorney and told him I wanted to fight the banks. We decided that we would send a strong letter to the state agency which regulates and investigates commercial banking procedures.

After a month or so I received a copy of their answer through my attorney, in Albany, New York. They had investigated and decided that the bank showed no evidence of redlining. I still believe that the bank did an excellent job of covering-up. We also learned that there was no law against age discrimination because of youth. Only in cases of discrimination against the elderly could they intervene. I was astounded, defeated, and my ego shattered. To this day, I feel there should be a law against discriminating because of youth.

That deal was only one of many disappointments in my new career. I had made a string of excellent purchases and now I was hitting a lot of roadblocks, especially in the area of finance. It seemed as if every area was a dead end for more seed capital.

4 See Appendix.

Momentum

Two months had passed since I had finished the renovation of the six-unit at 16 Eagle Street. One day, I called the tax office to ask some questions about the bills on several properties. I was speaking to the supervisor, and during our conversation, we began talking about how unusual it was for someone of my age to own so much real estate. In the course of our conversation, he told me he had a four-unit building on Swan Street that he wanted to sell. This caught my interest because Swan Street was only two short blocks away from my five-unit, two four-units and six-unit on Eagle Street. We agreed to meet at 20 Swan Street and inspect the property. He was sincere, honest and truly a nice person.

There was no facade or tough approach with him. He took this building on as a hobby several years earlier. He loved painting, plumbing, electrical work and carpentry. This type of work was relaxing for him. Fred was very meticulous about his work, too. Everything he did was exacting and right to code. To give you an example, he had two brand new hot water heaters hooked up. One worked and supplied more than enough hot water for the building. The other was an auxiliary and he was really proud of it. If the one wasn't working, the other kicked on so there would be no chance of the building being without hot water. Except for painting the exterior, the work was almost complete.

Fred didn't need a lot of money up front. He just had other projects now and didn't want to be bothered with the responsibility of managing the building. I told him how I bought the other buildings two blocks away for $25,000, with only $2,500 down, and the five-unit for $2,850 out of pocket, just to prepare him for a low offer. I made it sound like a regular offer by using those comparisons. When a fellow like Fred takes extreme pride in a property, you must never insult him. This type of person would rather give the property away than be badgered or insulted into selling. We were at a $24,000 sale price with $2,500 down, and I just could not get him any lower. Finally I tried a move I had learned through a "how to" book. I said, "Fred, instead of $24,000, how about if I give you $25,500?" Boy, did Fred perk up! "Why would you do that?" he asked. I pretended to be embarrassed, and told him very humbly that it would really cut me short if I had to come up with $2,500 down. I'd be willing to give him more money in a sale price if he would only take $1,500 down. Fred said that he wanted to think about it and talk it over with his wife. I sure didn't want to lose this deal. It was a steal at $2,500 down. I just kept thinking all the way home that I was getting too greedy. Why was I pushing it? Fred was real touchy about his hobby, and I didn't want to risk losing the purchase.

The phone rang that evening. I stood my ground and won. In the end Fred won also, as I'll explain later. The only stipulation was that the sale be in the form of a land contract.[5] This simply meant that the deed would not be transferred to me until the mortgages were satisfied.

I came across 8 Hawk Street, a three-unit building in the Multiple Listing Service. Al Knight, the owner, was a part time Realtor and had listed this property several months earlier. The price of $23,000 seemed below market and the assumable mortgage of $17,781 at 7-1/2% was quite attractive. The other drawing card was the location. Hawk Street was located between Eagle Street and Swan Street, where most of my properties were located. Al Knight was very anxious to sell his three-unit. He had bought a farm about 80 miles from the property and did not want to travel to Schenectady to maintain the building anymore.

He hadn't kept up with the maintenance, either, and had to sell it now or put some money into it. Lucky for me that he was smart enough to realize that!

As Al took me through each of the units, he pointed out many of the cosmetic deficiencies. He did such a good job of it that I did not need to say a word. Al picked the building apart and was actually selling it lower and lower without even realizing it.

After the inspection, Al and I talked for quite a while about his previous investments and why he was dissolving his income properties. I then told Al my age, which impressed him, and my story about all the properties I had gathered thus far. In the course of our conversation, I also dropped some hints about my being a little low on investment capital at the moment. I told him I would really like to have his property, but that now wasn't a very good time, just to test his anxiousness to sell. I don't think he had any offers on the property in the several months that it had been listed.

It seemed to me that this property had all the ingredients for my second "no money down deal." During our conversation I became aware of the fact that Al was a security conscious fellow. He did not necessarily need cash, but he would want some type of assurance that the payments would be made and the building kept in good repair.

When Al balked at my no money offer, I convinced him to go over one block to Eagle Street and have a look at some of my other properties. As we looked at the exteriors, I could see Al beginning to weaken. I had won this round, but not the whole battle. I had a very good rapport with just about all of my tenants. When there was a problem they knew they could count on me. With this in mind, I tried to close the deal. I asked Al if he would like to see some of the interiors and talk with a few of the tenants. He called my bluff and we went.

After the third tenant, I asked Al if he would like to go through a few more just to be sure these tenants were being truthful. But Al had seen enough.

Needless to say, the tenants gave me excellent reviews, and Al was impressed. "I wish I had started at your age too," he told me. That's when I knew I had won.

The only problem with no money down was the fact that the property was listed with the real estate agency and a commission had to be paid.

He was the listing agent so he would get a portion of the commission. Even though I was buying the property, I still had my real estate license, so I was entitled to the selling commission. I agreed to give up my commission to his office for a "no money down" purchase. I also agreed to accept responsibility for the security deposits, so he would not have to pay me at the closing. The final agreement was a purchase price of $23,000. I would assume $17,781.02 at 7-1/2%. He would hold approximately $5,000 at 10% for 10 years. NO MONEY DOWN! The total monthly payment was $205. Total rents were $550 per month, plus $30 for rental of the two-car garage. Taxes totaled a little less than $100 per month. Net monies to me were about $300 a month. For no money down, I would realize almost $3,600 per year.

This was one of my favorite purchases. I had very few problems with 8 Hawk Street, and my profit when I sold it a year and a half later was a handsome one.

The 8 Hawk Street deal closed November 3, 1979. On November 5, just two days later, my wife and I closed on 812 Grant Avenue, as well. I was going to celebrate my 24th birthday this month and wanted to finish the year as strongly as I had started it.

I had been negotiating 812 Grant Avenue, a brick two-family house, for several weeks. The property was listed in my real estate office by another associate. The woman who listed it approached me because word had spread about my purchasing a lot of properties in that area. This building was right around the corner from my very first purchase, 455 Hulett Street.

She told me that the owner was very anxious to sell. He was tired of being a landlord and did not want to spend any more time or money repairing the property . The asking price was $15,000. Sh felt sure he would hold some paper, too.

Why Some Landlords Fail

Before I continue, I would like to clear up some questions that all of the "Doubting Thomases" who read this will have. The first question, of course, would be: How could the asking prices and purchase prices be so low? The second excuse for not getting started might be: These must be slum properties and I could never handle that type of property or tenant.

I will take these objections, or better yet, excuses, one at a time. These questions can probably be answered with my philosophy about people. This includes rich, poor, black, white, Spanish, Chinese, Indian, upper and lower socioeconomic and any other classification one can pinpoint.

Clarification: The lower priced purchases of 455 Hulett Street, 335-337 Hulett and 812 Grant Avenue were in what might be called a marginal area. In Schenectady there are no real slum areas, so to speak. This area is where many low income families live. However, upon close scrutiny, one will find it contained working and middle income families as well. The neighborhood had deteriorated since its original inhabitants of doctors, lawyers and other professional types had moved to the suburbs. The city government started pumping]in federal and rehab funds. The only way it could go now was up. Along with help and upgrading by private individuals like myself, any investor can cash out of these properties quite profitably.

But, getting back to my philosophy on people. There will *always, as long* as we're a free society, be people earning small incomes. That is a fact. I tried it, I lived it, I experienced it. Do you know what happens when you dare to give these people decent housing? I'm talking about nothing more than paint, Pinesol, a little carpet, clean yards, washers in the leaky faucets, and patches on the holes in the walls. When you show them that you care about your property, which, by the way, is their home, when you take some pride in it and listen to their gripes and sincerely try to take care of them, guess what? They will treat that property like their own. It's contagious. Just because people are poor, it does not mean they don't have pride. That is why they will destroy the landlord who treats them like less than himself. I've seen it over and over. I've seen property right next to mine deteriorate because the tenants resent only seeing the landlord on the first of the month for the rent.

Landlords of that caliber disgust me. When I hear this type of person complain about tenants, I smile. It makes me happy, because I know it won't be long until I get a bargain price on his run-down, mismanaged property. I salute you, slumlords, for helping me be successful and destroying your own chances.

I really don't mean to be cynical, but this point needs to be driven home. It is so inexpensive to replace washers in a leaky faucet, or patch a hole, yet it can make the difference between success and failure. Whether one does this work himself, or finds a handyman, as I did, it is the cheapest insurance around. Call it success insurance.

The next objection those "Doubting Thomases" will make is that prices in 1979 were a lot lower, and that it isn't possible to find such prices nowadays. Wrong again. I moved to Florida (I will fill in the details later) in February of 1982 and bought a seven-unit building for $75,000, with $4,700 down. I was offered $130,000 for it six months later. I also purchased a six-unit building in a very nice area for $200,000 with only $6,000 of my own money. So, it can still be done in 1992, 1993, 1994, and, probably, in 2094, as well. I will elaborate later on some of my other purchases in Florida.

But I'm digressing. Let me get back on track here. We were negotiating the terms on 812 Grant Avenue to close the same month (2 days later) as 8 Hawk Street. Since I don't remember the lady associate who brought the property to my attention, let's refer to her as Linda. I asked Linda to bring the owner to our office. I was becoming quite successful at putting my own offers through, so I wanted to approach the owner myself.

I met him the following day at our office. He worked for the phone company and was about 40 years old. He seemed to have done fairly well for himself financially. He had a very nice house, owned a summer cottage and was very enthusiastic about camping, snow mobiling and several other outdoor sports. During our initial meeting, I learned that he dabbled in the stock market and had made some very good returns. Elwood had purchased 812 Grant Avenue several years ago. He maintained it fairly well over the years and used it for a tax write-off. He wasn't really adamant about needing a lot of cash from the sale. I figured that he just didn't have the time for it any longer and wanted to pursue other interests. After a pretty lengthy conversation about our mutual backgrounds, I presented my offer of

$8,000 with $1,000 down. I assumed his $4,247 first mortgage with 7 years left at 7% (contract for deed) and he held the balance of $4,500 in a second mortgage at 10% for 10 years. My total payments excluding taxes ($754 per year) and insurance ($129 per year) totaled $124 per month. The gross rents were $180 per flat, or $360 per month, with tenants paying their own utilities. My net profit per year would be approximately $2,000. Again, I made a 100% return on the invested cash in the first year.

I improved the cosmetic appearance of that property with some interior painting, minor landscaping and a few other inexpensive improvements. Comparative buildings on the block were selling and listed for sale between $18,000 and $34,000. After the upgrading, I increased the insurance on my properties at my agent's suggestion.

Within one year of purchasing this property, I ended up with about a 900% return on my initial investment of $1,250. The following December, there was a fire that almost completely destroyed the interior of the apartments. I finally settled with the insurance company for $18,000 in damages. With the proceeds, I paid off the $7,900 in mortgages to the bank and to the previous owner. This left me with $10,000 in cash to fix the property.

While I was pricing material, my handyman said he would perform some free labor for me if I gave him 812 Grant Avenue. I really didn't want to go through the hassle of fixing the property, so I agreed. He put five new ceramic tile baths in for me at some other locations and installed a new furnace at 8 Hawk Street, enabling all the tenants to pay for their own heat. I kept the $10,000. To top it all off, the $10,000 was not taxable as ordinary income.

Knowing About a "Public Adjuster" Netted Me $10,000

I would like to insert a paragraph here about insurance companies and claims. I had problems getting the insurance company to settle. They sent an adjuster out to meet me after the fire, and, being "young and inexperienced," I knew nothing of their methods. I answered all his questions about purchase price and terms honestly. As I eventually found out, this was the wrong way to handle this situation. Purchase price has nothing to do with value. I bought the property at a steal, to say nothing of all my improvements, labor, and material costs. Of course, even though I told the adjuster this, he never heard it. One day I happened to mention the fire to some friends. They had already gone through one and had a real problem getting their just due from the insurance company. They told me to call the Public Adjusters Corporation. This is an independent company that works for a commission (percentage of the claim) at settling insurance disputes for the homeowner. They do all of the dealing with the insurance company. They are pros at what they do and are well worth their commission. I would never have come out with $18,000 had I not hired them. Chances are I would have received less than $8,000.

Most people are not aware that these Public Adjusters exist. Many of them have radio equipment and tie into calls to the fire department. When you've had a fire, they send a regular salesman out to sell their service. Unfortunately, the average person thinks their insurance company will take care of them. Not true! Many insurance companies hire independent adjusters to handle the settlement. They try to get to you immediately before a Public Adjuster does. They dislike the Public Adjusters and will talk them down terribly. Don't be fooled. Insurance companies are big businesses and can be very impersonal. Their job is to collect premiums and pay as little as possible in claims. If you think differently, you're in a dream world. Take my advice and get an independent adjuster, especially when income property is involved. With all of the properties I own and have owned, Grant Avenue was the only fire I've ever had. Maybe I've been lucky, but I attribute this to the attention I give the properties. Whatever the reason, you can bet if I ever do have another fire, I'll let the pros negotiate it.

If you consider the subject from a logical standpoint, it makes very good sense. I compare it to having the best accountant or best attorney in town. If one can put the deals together then he should hire the best people in the various affiliated fields to carry out the details. That advice paid off nicely for me at tax time, as well as with the fire, as you'll soon find out.

If you recall, we were discussing my desire to end 1979 as strongly as it began. Well, the two closings in November sure helped me achieve that goal. Insurance damage money is not taxable. The money was free and clear.

My handyman fixed the property and eventually sold it for a $5,000 profit. Everyone made out well-especially me!

"What They Didn't Tell Me About Accountants"

I had no upcoming closings, so I spent December searching for a good accountant. Unfortunately, I did not prepare well that first year. We grew so fast that all of our records were kept in three-ring binders. We never did the monthly totals for each building, either. We had kept all of the receipts, income and expenses, but we hadn't done the monthly totals. I just thought the accountant handled all that.

Well, after some searching for a real estate accountant, my wife Ingrid and I finally settled on "Double X and Company. "Our first meeting was at his combination house and office in an exclusive suburb of Schenectady. There were several secretaries bustling around, the furniture and carpet were very plush and we were served wine in a crystal glass. I was very impressed with all of this and thought I was in good hands. I wish I had known then what I know now.

When I think back, I'm not quite sure how to evaluate fairly the job he did. My present accountant is both an attorney and a C.P.A. His opinion, leaving out various adjectives, is not particularly charitable. I was audited by the I.R.S. in 1981 because of the job Double X and Company did on my 1979 taxes.

I'll explain the audit later. What prompted it was this.

We took our average income over the previous three years when Ingrid and I worked at the slaughterhouse. We had so much shelter and depreciation now that he was able to recoup $7,000 in taxes that we had paid in 1976, 1977, and 1978. The government sent us back all that money PLUS 6% interest on the money for the time they had it. This part of his work was great, and we received those monies the following July of 1980. The negative part was his bill of $1,000.00. My present accountant says that was pretty high. I thought that it was acceptable at the time. I was in the big leagues now and expected to pay for it. Also, he did have to do all the totals and reorganize a shoe box full of receipts. The only place he made a huge error (in my opinion) was taking too quick a depreciation on the properties. This was the reason for the I.R.S. audit in 1981.

I remember the terror I felt on the day I opened the letter for the audit. I called my accountant and we started plotting our course of action. He's about 32 years old, very aloof, and very competent. His law background is quite helpful in many areas of accounting.

Our strategy was to stretch the audit out as long as possible, with as many meetings as possible. Wear out the auditor, so to speak. We were assigned to a woman, and she looked exactly like you would expect a woman auditor to look. I believe her name was Wilma McNasty, and she had the personality of an iceberg.

The letter was very precise about what books and records she wanted to see, but according to our strategy, my accountant went to the first meeting without me or any records. I'm sure this pleased old Wilma. My accountant played dumb and had her explain what we would need, and scheduled a second meeting for a month later. We were both to attend that one.

Actually, he didn't want me to attend this meeting. He felt it would be better to deal with the auditor alone for several reasons. The main one was my personality. I am rather blunt at times and specialize in snappy answers to snippy questions. I understand the Joe College attitude completely, but they don't generally understand me.

Growing up in a tough area of New York roughened my edges a bit, as did my lack of a college education. I was, however, gifted with the ability to read and comprehend. I have a library of hundreds of books and tapes that have educated me quite thoroughly in areas that are of importance to me. In general, I can understand the hostility I might arouse in a stranger. I have made a good amount of money, owned quite a bit of property and appear to be extremely successful at a very young age, but I can be lacking in diplomacy. Maybe we'll meet one day and you'll understand.

At any rate, my accountant did not want me to attend that second meeting. But being that stubborn, unsophisticated boy from New York City, I insisted. I figured if I was going to grow and the I.R.S. was going to haunt me, I wanted to meet them head-on and learn everything I could about the way they deal. For the second meeting, we purposely left several of the requested records at home again. It was my accountant's hunch that Mrs. McNasty's boss would be giving her grief about clearing her caseload. If we stretched it out long enough, she would close the case just to get rid of it. Eventually, that is exactly what happened. Also, even though I had taken too rapid a depreciation, I still had enough shelter to cover most of the adjustment.

The end result, after several weeks of sitting on pins and needles waiting for the decision was: Tax return accepted as filed.

Internal Revenue Service
District Director

Department of the Treasury

Date: NOV 9 1981

Return Form Number:
1040
Tax Periods Ended:
12/31/79
Person to Contact:
B. Sadlonill
Contact Telephone Number:
(518)472-7666

Russell & Ingrid Whitney
3160 Guilderland Avenue
Schenectady, New York 12306

We are pleased to tell you that our examination of your tax returns for the above periods shows no change is required in the tax reported. Your returns are accepted as filed.

If you have any questions, please contact the person whose name and telephone number are shown above.

Thank you for your cooperation.

Sincerely yours,

John B. Lange
District Director

cc: Charles E. Miller
15 Loudon Parkway
Loudonville, New York 12211

Clinton Avenue & North Pearl Street, Albany, N.Y. 12207

Letter 590(DO) (Rev. 7-78)

Chapter II

Getting Off Track Can Be Costly

I became involved with a sales organization that was set up to purchase merchandise directly from the manufacturer at cost prices. As a result, the consumer was able to save large amounts of money on purchases. I eventually purchased a territory (like a franchise) and invested the remainder of my real estate "seed" capital.

There was tremendous potential in the concept of being able to buy directly from the manufacturer, eliminating the "middleman" profit. However, there were some disenchanted members in the organization that caused some legal problems for the owner. These various problems ultimately led to negative publicity and the eventual demise of the company itself.

I lost the $12,000 investment I had made, but the real hurt came when I thought of what I could have done had I invested that cash in some more real estate.

There is positivity in the situation if you consider the fact that I learned a great deal about sales. This has helped catapult my real estate holdings today. However, the fact still remains that I was off track and should have never stopped investing in real estate.

In the final analysis, I lost a whole year as well as the $12,000. I lost it because of my ego and pride. Let the buyer beware (*caveat emptor),* especially when you accumulate some cash and assets! There will be plenty of bad opportunities, as well as good ones.

In the course of my reading education, I have found that almost all of the successful individuals in history have had many failures on the road to success. Thomas Edison tried over 1,000 experiments over the course of many years before he found the right filament to make the light bulb work. Do you think he was tired of trying? Perhaps, but that's what determines the difference between a winner and a loser. Thomas Edison's attitude and success are reflected in his statement about his failures. He said he didn't fail at all. He just found 1,000 ways that the light bulb *wouldn't work!* I could quote many statements from successful people that reflect the same undying positive attitude, but I'll spare you. Just remember that the winners in life make it happen. The losers in life just let it happen.

Understanding the First Vital Secret of Success

It only takes a few ingredients to turn a man's life around from mediocrity to success. Before I explain what they are, let's take a minute to talk about your future. By "future," I mean, starting from today. If you say, "I hope things will get better," you'll always be poor. You see, things aren't going to change. The world is going to stay pretty much like it's always been. The day will break, the sun will cross the sky, and night will follow. The tides will rise and fall. Sometimes the wind will blow and sometimes it will be still. Sometimes it will be stormy, and sometimes it will be calm. Sometimes things go well, and sometimes they don't. Sometimes people will delight you, and sometimes they will disgust you. Your surroundings aren't going to change radically. But for your future to get better, you've got to change. You've got to grow. *You've* got to get better.

It's easy to blame everything but yourself for all your problems. You could even come up with a list of reasons why you're not doing well. I bet it would be a darn good list, too. You might blame it on the weather. Several months during the winter are pretty tough. Maybe your parents are poor, and there wasn't anyone to help you get started. You were probably raised in the wrong part of the country, too, and didn't have a complete formal education. How can you make big money without a degree? I'll bet your relatives are always putting you down, and won't loan you money, either. I'll bet you even have neighbors that won't help you. That's a pretty good list of excuses for being broke. Can't pay your bills on time, no money left over at the end of the month. That's a heck of a good list. You could work on it for years.

I hope, though, one day you'll come to your senses and find out the truth about life. It's not what happens to a man that determines the quality of his life. You see, what happens, happens to everybody. The same things can happen to two different people, and one will turn it to a profit and the other will stay poor. So what's the difference? The difference is what you do about it! Somebody says "Yeah, but you don't understand the problems I've had." *Come on,* everybody has disappointments in life. The difference is how you look at them. Attitude. That's what can turn a mistake into a learning experience, a set-back into a challenge, and, ultimately, failure into success. It's how you feel about what happens to you that makes the difference.

Now, here are three ingredients to give you the attitude for success. These ingredients could turn today one of the greatest days of your life.

1) Number one is *disgust.* Sometimes that's what it takes to really start making some changes. Disgust with poverty and its embarrassment, disgust with mediocrity, disgust with just getting by, disgust with not being able to pay the bills on time, disgust with having to deny yourself and your family things they really need. You finally need to reach to point where you've had it. . . right up to here! When a man has had it with niggling about poverty, a day finally arrives when he says it and means it. *I have had it.* When your wife goes to the supermarket and she's looking at two cans of beans, one for forty-nine cents and one for forty-seven cents, you know which one she's going to buy. She's going to buy the cheaper one to save two pennies, and she doesn't even like the brand! That's when it's time to say, "I have had it!" To finally start turning your life around, you've got to be weary of how it has been. You've got to get disgusted.

2) Here's the second ingredient-*decision.* You need to decide what you want out of life. If you want to change, decide and get on with it. And if you want to keep the momentum going, you have got to learn to make *quicker* decisions. Do you know what indecision is? Indecision is a thief of opportunity. Indecision will steal you blind. Indecision will clean out your bank account. Indecision is a habit that stems from fear. Fear when you know you're on the fence but are afraid you'll get off on the wrong side. Here's the tragedy of sitting on the fence—while you sit there, the clock keeps on ticking. Life will pass you by, and life is the most precious thing you've got.

I was on the phone the other day with a friend of mine in New York. I asked him what he was doing these days and he said, "Oh, just working and killing time." I said, "Oh no! don't do that!" Poor guy only has a little and he's killing part of it! Don't do that. Make the minutes count. That's why you should learn to make quick decisions. Just get off the fence. It really doesn't matter which side. Remember, a life full of adventure and achievement is a life full of many decisions. The ones that turn out wrong make you strong, and teach you to make better decisions. Don't see how many decisions you can get out of, see how many you can get into. And learn to speed up the decision-making process. It will add many full and satisfying years to your life.

3) The third ingredient is *action. In th*e final analysis, you have got to act. You can work your way through *disgust* and *decision*, but in the final analysis, to change direction, you've got to act! That is what makes your desire a reality. It means accepting the responsibility for your own life. For things to change, *you've* got to change. For things to be better, you've got to be better. It's called personal growth. Don't blame external things for the problem. Look inside yourself for the solution.

Here's an anecdote that says it all about the failing man looking for an answer from the Universe.

The man cried, in desperation, to the Universe, "Give me more time," and the Universe answered, "There is no more time, give me more you!"

Find out how to get more value out of yourself. Don't just stumble along, just trying to find the money to pay the bills. Don't settle for mediocrity. Learn as you go through the day. Watch with interest. Wherever you are, be there! Don't let success pass you by without scrutiny. Look it over, think about it and then make it your own.

The first step to personal growth is to find out how things work. Step number two is: go to work. First get the knowledge, then apply it.

Just look for three or four things that can improve your life and your economic future. Just find three or four things and then go to work on them like crazy. Let me add a word of caution here. Don't wait until you have three or four thousand things. Do you know why? You'll use up all of your time analyzing, and you'll wind up smart . . . and broke. It's okay to be dumb and broke, but if a guy is smart and broke, it's pitiful. Don't let your learning lead to a dead end. Let your learning lead to action, and you could get rich. ACT!

I really did not want to stray from real estate investment too much, but there is a way of thinking that a person must understand before he can ever be successful. I learned many of these things while I was involved in sales. I learned about failure and I learned about people. And that helped me learn how to make money.

During that year with the sales organization, I lost many real estate opportunities. I did take advantage of a few, though, that I'd like to tell you about.

Knowing What to Look for Made Me $5,000 in One Hour

I found 813 and 819 Lincoln Avenue in the "income property for sale" section of our local paper. I knew the area very well. It was a few blocks from my three Hulett Street properties. Lincoln Avenue was about the worst street in that neighborhood, since the owners had let the properties run down. There were some decent buildings, but not many.

I called the owner, and made arrangements to meet him for a visual inspection. The properties were in disrepair. Most of the needed work was only cosmetic, but there was a lot of it to be done. The properties were two-family houses consisting of 3 bedrooms per flat. There were a total of four units, and the rents were reasonable for the condition of the houses. The asking price for each house was $12,000.

As the owner and I talked, I found out why he was selling. His wife was the actual owner of the property. Her former husband had bought them originally, and when they separated, he dumped them on her. She really knew nothing about being a landlord. She would just hire licensed contractors for repairs, and her husband was tired of dealing with them. As always, I explained my "story" about my other real estate holdings, and my ability to improve these "losers." I told him that his price was a little high, but that I might be able to make some type of offer. I promised to call him that evening to let him know my decision.

Ingrid and I discussed the properties that evening. We decided that if we were going in super low, it would be better if we both went to his house to sell him and his wife on our stability and ability to handle the properties. When I called him that evening, I told him I really didn't want to discuss the offer over the phone. That paved the way for him to invite us to his house the following day.

Ingrid and I arrived that evening at a very nice house in a suburb of Schenectady. He and his wife were very hospitable. We chatted with them for quite some time and talked about generalities to set them at ease and establish trust. When we finally brought out the written offer, there was a prolonged silence. We were offering $7,500 per building with $500 down apiece: a total package price of $15,000 with $1,000 down. They would hold the mortgage of $14,000 at 9% for 10 years. Our payment would be $142 per month. All four units were rented for $150 per month. Gross rents per month were $600 The taxes for both properties totaled $100 per month ($50 apiece), and the tenants paid all utilities. With some rent raises, we would net about $5,000 per year.

It is very important not to be cocky with such an offer. It must be sold as your *inability* to come up with more cash. Never browbeat your "opponent." Be humble and ask for help. I guarantee that the percentages will be with you.

They accepted the offer. There was a lien on the properties which needed to be cleared up, so we set the closing for three months later.

Before I finish the story of Lincoln Avenue, I must fill you in on what happened during the three-month lapse before we actually closed.

The Circumstances That Netted Me $5,000 for an Hour's Work

I met Dan through my sales organization escapade. Dan was very successful in the same organization, and had worked with the company before I became involved in it. At the age of 22, he earned in excess of $30,000 in sales for this company. He even increased that figure the following year. Dan sensed the impending legal problems I mentioned earlier and eventually quit. He then worked as a stockbroker for Merrill Lynch and eventually opened a grocery store in the area, which was also very successful for him.

I met Dan just before I left the sales company. Dan and I evaluated our future there and decided we had a lot in common. We discussed forming a partnership with either real estate properties or some type of business.

I believe it was March or April when Dan and I decided to go to Florida and investigate some investment opportunities.

Why Florida? In upstate New York, not only is it miserably cold, but my properties did not seem to be appreciating naturally. All of the appreciation was forced through improvements. Florida real estate was increasing in value naturally. I thought that if I was going to make this my career, then I should be where the growth is. New York was actually losing about 4% of its population per year, while Florida was, and is, growing by leaps and bounds.

We mixed pleasure with business during our trip, but set our work schedule during the 1500 mile drive. Since I had already seen most of the east coast of Florida on previous vacations, I was more interested in investigating the west coast. I also had to find an older city in Florida with distressed properties. We looked in just about every major city on the east coast before cutting across Alligator Alley in south Florida and heading towards the Gulf of Mexico.

Dan's uncle knew and dealt with a Realtor in a town in southwest Florida called Cape Coral. The Realtor had been buying and selling vacant lots for Dan's uncle for about six years and had turned considerable profits for him. His uncle recommended that we meet this Realtor upon our arrival. As our journey toward the Cape Coral/ Fort Myers area progressed, we were astounded with all of the new construction that was going on.

Cape Coral was a vacant 100 square miles of scrub land near the Gulf of Mexico in 1958. It is now the second largest city (in land area) in the state, second only to Jacksonville. Apparently the developers had tremendous foresight regarding the future of Southwest Florida. They dug over 400 miles of navigable canals which will take a boater from his backyard right out to the Gulf of Mexico. All of the lots were cleared and roads put in.

The town was developed to hold a population of some 500,000 people. The present population was approximately 60,000. What an embryo opportunity! The town and area are among the fastest growing in the nation. The year-round temperature is around 76 degrees, which attracts thousands of tourists and millions of their dollars.

The city of Cape Coral borders Fort Myers, which is the type of older city that I was looking for. As a matter of fact, Thomas Edison had a winter home and laboratory in Fort Myers right next to Henry Ford's home for many years.

So far so good. Our excitement grew tremendously upon meeting the Realtor. He had an ultra modern office in Cape Coral with 50 employees.

The Realtor had lived in Cape Coral for 16 years, and as we later learned, was in the millionaire status. He got started with the original developer of Cape Coral as a salesman selling lots and a dream to Northerners. It was a very lucrative business, since every lot (80 x 125) in the 100 square miles has been sold at least once. Waterfront properties were selling for $8,000 to $10,000 dollars in 1970-1975. They now begin at $100,000 in the more densely populated areas.

On our tour of the area, we learned that there were still many miles of empty waterfront lots which sold at 1970-1975 prices. Eventually these would climb to $100,000.

The excitement was killing us, and the more he talked the more we were sold.

He told us he had a deal on 12 lots, which we could buy for $24,000 with $9,000 down. We would send him $3000 apiece when we returned home and the other $3,000 would fall due in 120 days. Believe this or not, his office would guarantee us at least a 25% return on the invested cash in one year and one day. Apparently, he would sell the lots at that time for the profit, or his office would buy them.

We each wrote him a check for $100 as an earnest money deposit. The Realtor also was selling us on moving to Cape Coral for the opportunity there. He had moved there 17 years ago and obviously had done well. He even offered to help us get started in real estate and in new construction. New construction seemed to be the most lucrative opportunity with all the growth in the area.

We didn't make any decisions, as we still had several hundred miles of the west coast to investigate on our way back north. Our only decision was to buy those twelve lots.

We also had other points to consider. Dan had a thriving grocery store in New York worth a quarter of a million dollars, which earned him upwards of $100,000. a year. I had 13 or 14 apartment buildings with a rent roll upwards of $100,000 annually. We just couldn't walk away from that. Why should we? It was easy street, financial freedom, established respect in the community, and rapport with the banks. We had a womb of security, so to speak. Why should we risk all that for a mere possibility of success? Let me tell you why.

We left Cape Coral and Fort Myers and headed north through Sarasota, Tampa, St. Petersburg and Clearwater. We stayed in each city and talked to many Realtors before making the journey back to New York. As we headed home and talked about the trip there was no question in our minds that if we were ever going to move to Florida,

Cape Coral or Fort Myers was where we would go.

I guess it was around North Carolina or Virginia that we had to turn the heat on in the car and put on a sweater. I'm not really sure if it was just our eye contact or if we actually said anything at all to each other, but when the silence broke our decisions were made simultaneously.

"Let's get the hell out of New York!" We both agreed that it was a dying situation, with zero growth.

Sure, we were making money, but how could we truly enjoy it with nine months of sub-zero temperatures and two feet of snow? Heating bills were incredibly high and it was next to impossible to do any exterior maintenance all winter. There were numerous other reasons, including the possibility a of bigger success in a growing area of the country, namely, southwest Florida.

Now, all we had to do was convince our wives to give up the security, and reconcile them to moving away from friends and family. Dan had been married for about seven years, and I, six. It would definitely be a little easier for Dan, since he had no children and only one business to sell. I had 14 buildings and two children. My wife had lived in the area, as did Dan's wife, Adele, all their lives. Ingrid's mother, father and three sisters still lived in the area. If you have ever tried to move your wife 1500 miles from all of that security for the uncertainty of pie-in-the-sky success, then you know what we were in for.

Keep in mind, now, how average people think. Keep in mind the phrase I mentioned earlier. "For every one person who says it can be done, twenty (or even 100!) will say it can't."

When we finally returned home it was freezing and snowing like crazy. What luck!

The next day we approached our wives in a joint meeting on the subject. They were enthusiastic and very positive about the move. It was a unanimous decision.

Now came the time to implement our decision. Dan had to sell a $250,000 business. I had 14 buildings to sell, two of which I hadn't even closed on yet (12 and 819 Lincoln Avenue). In April of 1981, it was a buyer's market.

We set our goal to move for the following September, 1981. This gave us each six months to dissolve our holdings, which we believed to be plenty of time. Talk about pressure! I was low on capital because of my questionable investment in the sales company, and had to come up with $3,000 for the lots in Florida to boot! At this point, Ingrid and I had about $3,500 or $4,000 in the bank. The Lincoln Avenue closing was coming up and I needed $1,500 for closing costs and a down payment there. Oh, brother!

I became a bit nervous and wary of making such an uncertain investment with practically all the cash my wife and I had. I began to consider backing out of the lot purchase in Florida. There were several reasons for that decision.

First of all, I believed that the successes I had encountered up to that point were due to the fact that I controlled my own investment. In other words, I saw the property, knew the property, and negotiated the deal, either by myself, or in conjunction with the Realtor. My only serious failure so far was when I put $12,000 into the sales organization.

The broker in Cape Coral was Dan's contact. I didn't know Dan's uncle or any details of his dealings with Steve. I only knew what Dan had told me. Don't get me wrong. I trusted Dan completely. My only concern was that we knew this guy for a few short days and he had us sending him nine grand for some lots we'd never seen, 1500 miles away. It was a bit risky, wouldn't you agree?

Since the broker was Dan's contact, I called Dan and discussed my position on the deal. I felt I could put the $3,000 to better use locally. Dan both agreed and disagreed with me. He agreed it was risky, but felt that his uncle was a pretty shrewd businessman and would not deal with a dishonest person. Dan also was adamant on preserving the contact in Florida. If we were to move, this fellow could be a very important asset to us.

Finally, it turned out to be just a money decision, coupled with a little buyer's remorse. I didn't have the cash to spend. Dan was cash rich then but couldn't afford the whole nut by himself.

He called the broker and graciously explained the situation and asked him to get him into a lot purchase that would require a little less cash, as he would be purchasing the deal himself. I forfeited my $100 deposit and he got Dan into two lots elsewhere.

As it turned out, the broker found some other investors for the twelve lot purchase. The sad part (for us) is that he purchased it for them at the same terms of $9,000 down and a $24,000 purchase price. Then he sold it for them less than nine months later for $60,000 cash!

We would have made a $36,000 profit minus our $9,000 down. It was a wrong decision that cost us $25,000. One year later the broker sold Dan's two lot purchase for a $14,000 profit.

Why am I including the details of this spectacular mistake? I could have ended my story with all of my successes in the first year. The reason is simple. This is a real story, absolutely unexaggerated and accurate financially. I want you to understand that there is no easy way to make a lot of money. There is no road to success without some hurdles. If there was an easy way, I'd be doing it. When I say it's not easy, that doesn't mean the average person can't do it, because he can. You can! Why? Because it's simple. Not easy, but simple. I've said that a few times already because it is important that you remember it. Success means long hours and hard work. Rare are the people who inherit the big money.

Success and failure are facts of life. Everyone fails occasionally, including me. You just have to try to make the good decisions outweigh the bad. You not only learn something from the bad ones, but, if you look hard enough, you can even find a positive side to them. If you disagree, picture two men driving down an old country road on a beautiful sunny day. John says, "Boy, it's a beautiful day, isn't it, Ralph? The trees are in bloom, and the grass is so green this time of year. Boy, I just can't believe how warm it is today." Then old Ralph replies, "I know. My hay fever is killing me and I'm sweating buckets. Do you have to hit every bump in this road?" One man sees the positive side and the other sees only the negative. What do you think his chances of happiness and success are? Not many.

Well, I did make the wrong decision by not buying those lots, but I did find the positive side of that wrong decision. Now I was totaly convinced of the monies that could be made in Florida.

The months to come would be full of hard work trying to market all of my properties. My first goal was to sell the two Lincoln Avenue properties. Remember, I still had not even closed on these properties yet.

Mike and Jim were my wife's childhood friends. They bought one of the houses, which they shared when not working at their regular construction jobs. Mike in particular, had watched our real estate investments develop and our standard of living increase dramatically since Ingrid and I were married, just a few short years ago. He had attended our wedding and he and I had grown to be good friends. I had talked to him several times about getting started with a small investment or two, but he never pursued anything. I had just chalked him up to being one of the many people who work 9:00 to 5:00 and are content with that lifestyle.

I was certainly surprised that day in May, just a few weeks after I returned from Florida. He called me and told me he and Jim had decided to get into a few real estate investments. I thought that was great and we discussed some possibilities.

When we finally got around to discussing the Lincoln Avenue properties, I decided these would be the best deal for them. I had contracted to buy those particular properties for $15,000 with $1,000 down. They would be closing the following month, on June 3rd. They needed painting and cleaning up, and some interior work. Basically, all the work was cosmetic.

Now, before I detail how we structured the sale, I want you to keep some pertinent facts in mind. My long hours of looking for bargain properties, plus what I learned about negotiating (even from the bargains I lost), had enabled me to get the great terms on the Lincoln Avenue properties. That effort had to be worth something. When I negotiated the sale with those guys, I told them exactly what my price and terms were. It really didn't matter, because the deal I gave them would still give them almost a 100% return on their invested cash in the first year. They bought the properties on June 3rd, one hour after I closed on them. My terms with the seller were a $15,000 sale price with $1,000 down. I sold to them *one hour* later for $20,000 cash to mortgage. They assumed my $14,000 note to the seller, paid me my $1,000 down payment back and I walked from the closing with a $5,000 profit! The sellers were happy to get rid of the properties. Mike and Jim were happy to get the deal, and I was happy to make $5,000 for my efforts. One hour is about the shortest period of time that I've ever owned a piece of property, and probably the most fun!

Finding Out About the "Motivated Seller"—the Hard Way

I still had lots of buildings to sell before we could move and that's where some of the trouble began. It is bad to be in a position of the motivated seller. It goes against all the principles of being a good real estate investor. We *look* for motivated sellers. We spend hours and days trying to search them out for the good deals. Doesn't it make sense that to be in that position as an investor could be harmful? It does and I knew it.

I advertised my properties in two smaller package deals and in one big package. I would sell either way. I didn't want to start breaking them up individually. I had some offers but most were from investors who had got wind of my wishes to leave the area. They were ridiculously low and I didn't even seriously consider them. I had decided already what my bottom line was and I was determined to get it. I had at least a ten thousand dollar profit tacked on to each of the buildings, which wasn't unreasonable. They were all in good condition and I had put a lot of the rent money back into them for improvements.

One investor, in particular, had really hung in and kept after me to sell to him. He had cash and knew I was getting nearer to my deadline date to move. (Gabe, you know who you are!) I believe he and I were about $15,000 off in the price. In the interim, I had approached Mike and Jim about buying some of the properties I had left. They wanted them, but didn't have the cash.

One day I met a young investor (23 years old) whom I shall call John. The reason I call him John is that my honest description of him could not be printed. John had just recently graduated from college and his mommy and daddy had given him quite a large sum of money to get him started in real estate investing. He had already bought several run down properties and was fixing them up nicely. He had arranged some government rehabilitation loans and was moving right along. I met John at a bank foreclosure auction, which is how we had come in contact to discuss the sale of some of my properties.

Of course, John learned of my anxiousness to move and the negotiations started ridiculously low. As it turned out, we were still negotiating a year later. It must be obvious by now that we did not make our deadline of moving by September. When I look back on it, those goals were quite unrealistic, short of some miracle from heaven.

Dan was having a hard time selling his store, too. Finally, I mentioned the store to two of my brothers-in-law (the husbands of Ingrid's sisters). One of them, Floyd, was working at the slaughterhouse where I had worked several years earlier. It was bankrupt and would close its doors in two weeks. The other brother-in-law had spent the past ten years in and out of labor work, laid off sometimes for a year at a time. Needless to say, that is not a very prosperous life for a family with three children.

Dan and I both met with Floyd and Paul to discuss the possibility of their buying the store. The store was worth around a quarter of a million dollars and netted close to $100,000 or more per year. My brothers-in-law were used to earning anywhere from nothing to $20,000 in any one year. To make a long story short, Dan gave them a super deal with low money down. He trained and helped them get started, and they both are making a good living today in that store. Even more important, they also have the pride of being their own men in their own business.

This closing was in November. We were two months past our date to move and I still did not have a contract on my last seven properties. It was time to reschedule our departure date.

We decided to leave by January 29, 1982 and arrive in Florida by February 1, 1982.

John and one other investor seemed to be very near a final deal with me. Believe it or not, I thought at this time that John would be the more responsible party to sell to. The only thing that bothered me was that he was constantly changing his mind. We must have settled on a deal ten times. Then he would come back two days later and present something completely different. Unfortunately (and stupidly) I was clinging to this fellow as the means of selling my properties and getting started in Florida.

Controlling a $200,000 Property with $6,000 Can Be a Mistake

The month of Dan's closing on the store, I took Ingrid to Florida to show her where we'd be moving. Amazingly enough, neither she nor Adele had even seen Cape Coral yet! The reason for our visit to Florida was twofold. Ingrid wanted to see where she was moving to, and I was going to make some offers. I would either get a duplex, where both my family and Dan and Adele could live, or a bigger multi-unit property, for the same purpose. That would allow us time to research the market, plus give us a piece of income property when we decided to get our own houses.

I searched and searched for the next two weeks in Florida for a no money down deal in an area where we would want to live. Finally, I found a property that had just come out in a real estate magazine that day. It had never been advertised before. It was nine years old, and had six units, central air and heat, was carpeted, and had all the appliances, including a dishwasher. This was a prime property in a growing area of Cape Coral. I called and negotiated the purchase with the owner/broker, Robbie.

The listed price was $200,000 with three assumable mortgages totaling $155,000. I must admit this was a pretty big price for only six units. I had been used to paying $60,000 for a six-unit in New York. However, the property was in a prime area and I believed that $200,000 was somewhat below market value.

We met the owner/broker in a restaurant and negotiated the purchase right there over a cup of coffee. She was looking for $25,000 down and would hold paper on the balance, and we would assume the other mortgages. Even with $25,000 down we would still have a negative cash flow. This really went against my investment formula. Up to this point I had never bought a property with a negative cash flow. Our final deal was $12,000 down and a $198,500 sale price. The owner took back a $32,000 *interest only note* for 15 years. This note would have a $5,000 principal payment due every six months for three years. At that time, Robbie would be cashed out. Now our mortgages on the six-plex totaled $185,000.

This was a very good, "leveraged" deal. After the pro-rations at closing we would come up with a little less than $10,000 and would be controlling a property worth over $200,000. The bad news was the negative cash flow of $600 per month. We rationalized this negative cash flow as a disbursement that we would have to make if we bought separate houses, or rented upon our move. The deal was set to close (through the mail) on January 1, 1982.

Now we were definitely committed to move to Florida, and it had to be pretty near our goal month of January, or we would be managing a $200,000 property from 1500 miles away. We had also better start making some money when we moved because our first balloon payment[2] of $5,000 would be due less than one year from the January closing.

I'll explain later how we turned the negative cash flow and our $12,000 equity on the six-plex into $58,000 and a break-even cash flow, without ever making the first, or any, balloon payments to the owner/broker. By the way, at this writing, we still own the six-plex at 343 Cape Coral Parkway.

Needless to say, Ingrid and I returned to New York at the end of November extremely excited. We brought the pictures of our trip and our investment to Dan and Adele's house in Albany. We were all excited and couldn't wait to leave cold, snowy New York.

Amazingly enough, Dan put up half of the money on the six-plex without ever even seeing it. Of course, he did know the numbers.

1 See appendix. 2 See appendix.

More About the Motivated Seller

I now was working feverishly to finalize a deal on my last seven properties. Time was running out and John was still being difficult.

In late November, the two fellows who had bought my Lincoln Avenue properties called me and told me they had come into some money. They wanted to know if I could find them any other deals as good as the ones on Lincoln Avenue. They didn't have enough money to buy all of my remaining properties, although we really tried to put a deal together on them. We finally negotiated a suitable package on three of the remaining properties. I lowered the price and down payment and took back a mortgage for seven years. Finally, we arranged to close on January 29, 1982. This was the day we were to leave for leave for Florida. It pleased me that they were headed toward their own financial freedom using the same formulas and vehicles I had used.

More good news came early in December. John and I finally agreed on the terms for the purchase of my remaining properties, or so I thought. I conceded some on the down payment and we signed the contracts. There were a few small contingencies which I viewed as no problem at all. He was getting a super deal from a motivated seller. It was a deal I would have taken in a minute. We were all set to close on January 29, 1982. Finally, the pressure was off!

Everything would close early morning at my attorney's office on January 29, 1982. Then Dan and Adele, along with my family, would hop in the U-Haul and head our cars for sunny Florida. I remember that day distinctly. Dan and I rented the truck several days earlier. We helped each other load everything we owned into the U-Haul. Everything was ready the night before, January 28, 1982. I drove the truck to Dan's house. All the cars were gassed and ready to go. All that was left was for me to call the attorney, and go sign the papers.

I'll never forget the horror I experienced that morning when my attorney told me John refused to close that day. They were all set, but John, knowing I was the classic motivated seller, said there were some things his attorney still had to review.

We met at my attorney's office that morning and I was steaming. I had to leave that day for Florida! John assured me it was a minor detail and he would manage the property until we closed. We arranged for my accountant and attorney to handle the checkbooks and sign any checks, which needed both my accountant's and John's signature for bills. When rents were collected, they were to be brought to my accountant for deposit. Any maintenance monies were also to be disbursed by my accountant's approval at John's request. We left for Florida on schedule that day. I felt relieved to some extent, but I had a bad gut feeling about old John. Sure enough, I was right.

Six months later, we still had not closed. I was on the phone with my accountant constantly. I started getting some notices in the mail from the power company and several other creditors about past due bills. When I questioned my accountant, he said there were some extensive maintenance expenses, and we weren't showing much, if any, profit on the buildings.

Now I knew I was in trouble. I had lived totally and financially free off those rents for two years! They had to be showing a profit. If not, someone might have been stealing, or John was blatantly mismanaging the buildings. My accountant was controlling the checkbook and I knew he was honest, so where was the money going? And why hadn't we closed yet? Not getting any satisfactory answers and feeling like something terribly wrong was happening, or about to happen, I booked a flight on the next plane to New York.

How to Avoid Getting Ripped Off by Your Property Manager

I arrived in New York and went straight to my accountant's office to review the records of maintenance and the checkbooks. I could not believe what I saw! My accountant had disbursed monies to John that were absurdly high. There were checks made out for sums as high as $1,000 to $1,800. When I matched the bills to the checks, I found that John had all of the window ropes and weights replaced in an entire five-unit building! Needlessly, he also had wall-to-wall carpeting installed in several apartments. He had removed a bathroom sink to move it eighteen inches farther down the wall and replaced tub kits needlessly. Of course, his company performed the labor, which, based upon the bills, was probably the most expensive in the country. It was hardly what you would call good management for rental housing.

I also found records of vacant apartments, which, upon my inspection,were actually rented. I can only imagine how many rents were collected, pocketed and reported vacant. When I inspected the properties, there were only about five vacancies in a total of the 14 units I had left. I ran an ad that day and had all but one unit rented with full security deposits and a full month's rent by the end of that week.

I knew I was in trouble, so I started formulating a game plan. Most of that week, my time was spent between my accountant's office and the properties. I tried desperately to get a handle on the books and vacancies. I found three months of heating bills unpaid, which totaled close to $4000! There were countless errors everywhere.

The one unit I did not get rented was my house, which was the same house I initially re mortgaged to get started back in 1978. The house had well water and apparently the tenants had complained about the pressure being low. John never attended to the complaint and the pump started sucking sand into all the lines. The problem would have been easily remedied if a new point was driven. A small problem was allowed to become a major one. To add insult to injury, I could not convince the owner of the property behind my property to give me an easement so I could run city water in.

One day that week, I went over to meet with the two fellows who had bought the Lincoln Avenue property. They were keeping up the properties I had sold them very well. They had about 18 units in all now, all of which I had sold them. They were ready to buy some more and I felt that they had matured immensely since their first purchase on Lincoln Avenue one year ago. I was pretty confident they had the ability and desire to grow.

I discussed selling the rest of the properties to them and backing out of the disastrous deal with John. Unfortunately, (or perhaps it was fortunate) I was the position of the motivated seller. They didn't have a lot of cash, so I had to really concede with terms. I also dropped in price. The last of my properties sold for $143,000 with $10,000 down, and I took back a mortgage. It took another six months to close. Almost one year from the date we had moved elapsed before I finally cashed out.

During that time I took back all of the checkbooks and had all the rents mailed to me in Florida. Mike and Jim did the management until the closing and were paid 10% of the collected rents monthly. Presently, I get a very healthy mortgage payment from them every month and I will for the next 10 and 15 years respectively. Actually, that payment makes the payment on my house in Florida and covers most of our basic living expenses.

There is a definite lesson to be learned by the negative experience of selling those properties. I put myself in the position of the "motivated seller." Also, I put the complete management responsibility in the hands of a stranger and trusted him. He had no restraints on the management of rents and expenses. My accountant (who is very good at what he does) had no idea that the disbursements he made to John were out of hand. He didn't know the expenses that were incurred with income property. My guess is that John convinced him that those expenses were quite normal. It's true that as one's real estate investment portfolio grows, he must delegate responsibility to managers. I personally do so. However, I see and approve any expense above $100 on smaller properties. I will also look over the checkbooks at least once a month and talk to the tenants regularly.

That's one extraordinary point that I learned through my escapade with John. All of the tenants remained very loyal to me. I had such a good rapport with them that they totally resented and rejected John as the new buyer. Some were so elated to see me back in New York that I was astonished. I could actually see the wear, tear and abuse in several apartments that had not been there before. It was clear that they resented John and had taken out their frustrations on the property. What a pitfall for a new owner!

This game of real estate investment is a business involving homes and families. It could make anyone very wealthy if he remembers that the people, and his attitude are the key. It's worth remembering—people and attitude.

The "How-To" Book Never Mentioned Failure

So what was happening in sunny, southwest Florida during our first year there? We arrived on schedule, February 1, 1982. We each took one of the two bedroom, one bath units at the six-plex in Cape Coral. The weather was absolutely gorgeous. We had left New York under several inches of snow only two days earlier. Now we were at our new home and it was 80 degrees and sunny. We unpacked the U-Haul into our respective units, #2 and #5. We spent the next several weeks just exploring the area and relaxing in the sun.

Dan and I had planned to open up a small business upon our arrival, but couldn't seem to settle on a suitable choice. Everything seemed over-priced and unaffordable. My properties wouldn't be sold for almost another year, since we've backtracked one year in the story to our arrival in Florida. I only had about $5,000 cash to my name. All my money was still tied up in the properties. Furthermore, all of the rents, other than MHA3 (Municipal Housing Authority—government checks) were going to my accountant and John. I had, literally, no income at all.

Dan's store had closed smoothly. He received over $20,000 down and had $30,000 in the bank. His funds totaled $50,000, plus he had a healthy mortgage payment from the store of about $1,500 per month.

I didn't really feel pressured yet, though. I knew I could go out and find some properties, then arrange a home improvement loan to start rolling again. I started contacting Realtors, and going through the classified ads. I also ran my own ad, which had always worked well in New York. (I will give you a format for techniques and ads later in the book.)

Strangely, it seemed that I was hitting dead ends all the way. The market in Florida was completely different. Prices were at least double than what they had been in New York. I could not seem to get a positive cash flow anywhere, or find low or no down payment deals.

Dan and I kept looking. Early in our second full month in Florida, the broker who had sold Dan the lots found a steal on a single family house. It required $20,000 down and a price of $100,000. The house easily appraised for $130,000. Dan bought it and set a closing date for six months away. Then, shortly after, the broker sold Dan on a business venture which required another $25,000. This venture turned out to be a very long term deal for Dan. To date, he still has not seen a return. The money is secured with a piece of property, but he won't see any profit for some time. Now, Dan was running out of cash and we both felt pressured to get something going. Since we were not working and had only been in Florida for a few months, the banks would not even consider us for a loan. We continued searching for properties or a business and lived off our savings.

In March, a Realtor brought me a deal on a rundown, seven-unit building in downtown Fort Myers. Similar properties were priced at $100,000 to $150,000 in this area, even in poor condition. Up to this point, I had put in many offers with no acceptances. I offered $75,000 with $7,000 down and the owner to wrap[4] $68,000 at 12% for 30 years. To my amazement, it was accepted, with one small counter of a five year balloon.

I accepted, even though I only had $4,000 left in the bank and virtually no income. I offered Dan one half of the deal, which meant he would have to put up one half of the down payment. Unfortunately, he was low on cash now and couldn't do it. I started looking for an investor. At this point, I was desperate to get going again. I finally contacted my aunt and uncle in Reno, Nevada and explained the investment. For $3,500, I would give them one half of the tax shelter and one half of the equity upon a sale. I would keep all of the cash flow. Actually, this was a good deal for them. They needed a tax write-off, not cash flow, and their first year write-off would exceed $8,000. At closing, after pro-rations, I only had to come out of pocket with $4,700. This turned out to be a great investment.

I painted the outside with the extra cash we kicked in, had it tented for termites and immediately fixed up two of the apartments. The building at closing was occupied with less than desirable tenants and was being beaten to death. The rent roll was $1,075 per month, or $12,900 per year. Monthly mortgage payments totaled $703, with about $200 per month going to insurance and garbage pick-up. I had a small positive cash flow, but nothing phenomenal.

It was now February, and I had owned this property for a little under a year. I had used the rent monies, a little at a time, to carpet all the units, paint them, and furnish almost all of them. Our rent roll was $1,510 per month, or $18,100 per year. Our monthly net profit averages between $550 and $650. Also, I had been offered $130,000 to sell it. I would have had to give terms to sell, so I turned it down. I was building my portfolio again, so the asset looked good on my financial statement, and the cash flow felt good in my bank account.

Let's go back to March, when I initially purchased the seven-unit.

I was down to my last $1,000. The six-plex on Cape Coral Parkway was a big debt every month. Since we occupied two of the units, Dan and I had to compensate for those two rent losses monthly and that totaled $330 per unit per month. If you remember, we also had about a $600 negative cash flow. So we were paying about $600 to $700 per month, each, to keep it afloat. Now we were in trouble, especially me. Dan, at least, had his mortgage payment of $1,500 coming in monthly.

There was no choice for me. I had two children and a wife to support, so I started looking for a job to solve my immediate problem. After a million interviews, I finally found a sales job. My ability in sales was and is top notch after my co-op training. This was a job selling vending equipment on commission. I had to travel quite a bit around Florida, and had no guarantees. I lasted about 3 months before I got fed up with it and quit. I really wasn't getting or going anywhere.

It's amazing, but after you've tasted financial freedom you might as well forget about holding a job. I know now that I could never settle for that humbling experience again.

It was about this time, in June of 1982, that I made the trip back to New York to deal with the mismanagement of John. I was also cutting the deal with Mike and Jim on the remaining properties. Talk about pressure! I was broke. At least I got a $2,000 earnest money deposit from them and would have the rents coming to me again. That part went smoothly. I was paying all of the bills and sending them the monies they needed for management and maintenance.

Now that I was back in Florida, I continued to have the Realtor submit offers with little or no money down. Since I didn't have any money, there really wasn't much choice. The response was terrible. Whether it was bad salesmanship or that my offers were off track, I didn't know.

At this point, I was really getting discouraged. I questioned my formulas on no money down deals, and I questioned my ability to find opportunity here in Florida. I questioned my own work habits, too. Something had to be drastically wrong. I had been so successful in New York and here I was failing terribly. I just could not understand it.

I decided to get my real estate license. That way I would have an "in" on the local market and I could present my own offers. It also would be an opportunity for me to try and sell some properties for the commissions. It took some time, since Florida is a very tough state to get a real estate license in. Finally, I passed the boards and became an associate of a Realty company. It was the same company owned by the broker who initially raised our interest in the opportunity in Cape Coral.

Initially, I started prospecting and writing letters to possible investors. My strategy was to make some commissions and put some money in my pocket. With the real estate market and financing in the condition they were, many investors were holding back. My prospecting was not very successful, however. I was trying to deal in vacant lots, which were out of my area of expertise. I guess it took me about a month to finally get fed up. Finally, I drew some conclusions about myself. I had been flailing away at all these things that hadn't really made me any money at all. The times I had made big money and significant progress were when I was dealing in income properties. It was simply a comfortable and natural environment for me. So why was I messing around with all this other stuff instead of doing what I like to do, what I feel comfortable with and what makes me a bunch of money?

Would it have helped to make up a list of reasons for why I was not doing well? No, I already knew that wasn't the answer. I needed to know why the banks weren't dealing with me, or why my offers weren't being accepted, or even countered. I needed to know why I was in this rut, and, more important, how to get out of it.

3 See appendix. 4 See appendix.

What Does "Off Track" Actually Mean?

Some of this is new theory and some is old fact. I will speak in terms of sales, though these ideas directly relate to any independent business where one is his own boss and providing his own stimulus.

When I sat down and thought it out, I came to this conclusion. When a salesman or an investor like myself gets off track, he does not do so a mile at a time. If he did, it would be very noticeable and easily corrected. A person gets off track an inch at a time. Inch by inch, he drifts off course until he's finally off a mile. Let's say that a salesman has a presentation which his company has designed. They have spent many hours with top professionals to make sure the presentation consists of strong words and phrases. It also has pauses for buyer comments. They instruct the salesman to memorize his presentation and perform it verbatim. Past performance shows that the ratio of sales by each salesman has been best when it is done that way.

Instead of studying regularly to make sure he knows the presentation, the salesman forgets a little part. So, he injects a sentence or two of his own. It doesn't sound too bad and it's not much different from the verbatim presentation. Now he's off an inch. He's still selling, and at this point, being off an inch doesn't really hurt. But now he gets a little bored with saying the same things over and over again, so he adds a little here and makes a few changes there.

Little by little, he gets off track until he's actually off a mile. His sales are way down. If his sales are down, he's not making much money. Then what happens to his attitude? It starts to turn sour, and that throws him off track even more. Sales, just like investing, is a "people and attitude" business. Who wants to deal with somebody that's down in the dumps, feels lousy about himself and isn't making any money? People never crowd around a loser's locker room, do they? When I was a sales trainer for the co-op and a salesman's production was down, the first thing I would do was listen to his presentations. Most of the time he'd be way off.

What happens when you get off track? And, most important, what do you do about it?

Let's take those two questions individually. First of all, getting off track is like contacting a disease. The sooner you can detect it, the quicker you can affect a cure! The longer you wait, the more difficult it will be to start feeling like your old self again. And if you wait too long, it might even kill you. It can destroy your hopes, kill your dreams, and, at the very least, minimize your chances for success. You'll know when you're off track when:

1. You start questioning the product or service, instead of your own ability.

2. You start looking for someone else to blame because you're not making any progress.

3. You blame the economy for your present position.

4. You blame the banks.

5. You feel depressed and start looking to talk to someone else who is not doing well either.

6. You start looking for another field to get into because this one

doesn't work.

7. You start working later in the morning and quitting a little earlier in the afternoon.

8. You just don't want to make that next phone call because the guy you're calling will probably be in a bad mood. Even if he isn't in a bad mood, he probably won't sell his property for no money down. If he would sell it for no money down, it's probably in real bad shape, so the hell with it. You don't call him. You quit early and go play tennis.

9. You start seeing more negative things than positive things happening in your life.

10. In general, you stop doing the basics-the things you used to do when everything was going well. Even the little things.

The second question was, "What do you do about it?"

Actually, there are several things that can be done about getting off track. The best remedy is a preventative maintenance program. Simply stated, don't let yourself get off track. This can be curbed by constantly feeding your mind. Buy books and tapes that pertain to your field. Motivational and attitude tapes are also helpful. It's a funny thing, but people feed their bodies with food and drink every day, so they don't get tired, hungry or dehydrated. Well, your mind has to be fed, also. If you don't feed it with new ideas, with motivation and positivity, it will become stagnant. There are literally thousands of books and tapes in these fields. At the end of this book, I will give you a list of some of my favorites. I have hundreds of them, and the ones I list are some of the best on the market today.

Seminars are excellent for staying on track. I have been to many of them. My opinion is that, of real estate investment seminars, those by Mark Haroldsen of the National Institute of Financial Planning, are among the best. I have attended two of them in four years. The last one I attended was in January, 1983, and it was 1000% better than the one I attended in 1978. A number of excellent speakers participated, sharing their vast knowledge in many different fields of real estate investment.

As you are probably aware, I sat down and drew these conclusions about myself. I was really off track. It had happened a little at a time, but now I was off a mile. I had been tremendously successful in the early stages of my career, but now I had let all these little things get me totally away from the basics. I decided to do some things to correct myself.

First of all, I realized that my inability to secure any loans wasn't the fault of the banks. It was my fault. I was too out of sync to figure out why Florida bankers were different from the bankers in New York. Upstate New York is not very transient. The people have lived there for years, as did their parents and their parents' parents. Because of that, banks are much easier to approach for a loan. In Florida, the transience is tremendous. Many banks have been burned terribly with these types of people. I don't know why it had taken me so long to realize that.

Chapter III

Getting on Track:
"The $42,000 Payday"

Now I had to create a stable image of myself in the bankers' eyes. They like to see their loan applicants holding a steady job for at least a year, but I had no intention of ever getting another job working for somebody else. What did I do?

Since I had my real estate license with a Realty company, I was rendering my opinions on several of their commercial investments. Why not be the commercial property manager for them? In the banker's eyes, this is a salaried position. It's amazing, but I firmly believe that a banker would rather lend money to a guy who makes $250 per week as a laborer or a tradesman, than he would lend money to an investor like myself. He sees me as a wheeler-dealer type who could have his whole world come crashing down on him any minute. He sees the laborer as he sees himself. He works eight hours a day, pays the bills, might have a little money left over if he budgets. He doesn't realize that I have the ability to handle and nurture millions of dollars worth of debt. But, do I tell him this? No, of course not. I became the commercial property manager (by title) for an established firm.

The bank just loved that job on my loan application. As an added plus, the title showed I had experience in the field that I wanted to borrow in.

This took place sometime in November of 1982. It had been almost ten months since my move to Florida. I had made little gain or progress up to now. Little did I know that I was about to hit another winning streak with my new ventures.

I was a little pressured again, because we had a $5000 balloon payment coming due on our six-plex. The balloon was due in January, just two months away. Dan and I tried to market the property, but we had no takers. One day, while Dan and I sat talking, I came up with an idea. Since we had four mortgages on the property, why not try to do something with them?

The first mortgage was with a savings and loan at 7-1/2% with ten years left on it. The second was a $67,000 loan at 10% with 22 years left. The third was at 11% with 20 years left. The fourth was held by the broker who sold us the property. She was a pretty flexible seller, but her balloon payments would cash her out in three years. Her mortgage was for $32,000 at 12% interest only payments, with $5,000 due toward the principal every six months.

Here's what we did. Our savings were down to almost nothing. We called the second mortgage holder and simply asked him if he would take $45,000 cash immediately to satisfy the $67,000 mortgage. This constituted a 30% discount. Well, this fellow was about 62 years old and a 22 year mortgage would drag on for him. He thought it over and called us back the next day and said, yes, he would take the $45,000. We then called the third mortgage holder, and asked him if he would take $32,000 cash for his $45,000 mortgage. He called us a day or so later and said yes, as well. This was great! Now the fourth mortgage holder helped us tremendously by taking $22,000 for her $32,000 mortgage.

So far, so good. We went to the savings and loan that held the first mortgage. We explained our strategy to them and asked them to give us a new first mortgage of $142,000. This would turn their 7 1/2% mortgage into one with higher interest, plus they would put out $100,000 in new money on a safe loan secured by collateral.

After all of the red tape, we finally got a commitment. We also had all of the other mortgage holders sign an agreement the day after we initially called them. The agreement gave us 90 days to pay them off. If you ever use this technique, be sure to get a signed agreement from any and all mortgage holders so there are no foul-ups on closing day.

The end result was this: On closing day, the bank gave us $100,000. We paid off the mortgage holders in full and now had only one mortgage of $142,000. That little technique made us $42,000 in one day! There were some other benefits, too. The mortgage payments were $2,222 per month before. With the new bank mortgage, we reduced our payments to $1,600 per month. This gave us a break-even cash flow. We turned a $12,000 equity into a $58,000 (plus) equity just with a few phone calls!

Right now, there is an excellent opportunity to arrange for many of the same types of buy downs. You can arrange these on either larger or smaller scales. It is simply a "present value" concept. Can I make more money with X amount of dollars today, or will it be better invested over the next X amount of years with the present interest and terms? Most investors, I believe, would rather discount for cash.

If we look back a few years we can see why. When the banks started to tighten up, the only way people could sell their properties was by holding some of the mortgage for the new buyers. This was called "creative financing." Consequently, today there is a tremendous amount of paper being held by these sellers at 8-81/2% and 9-91/2%. We all know now that we could do much better if we had the cash to work with. This thing called "creative financing" has actually created more tools than ever for the investor who stays attuned to the trends.

That form of creative financing, (seller carrying back paper) is commonplace in today's market. Buy-downs are presently a new form of creative financing, as is the discounted paper for real estate acquisition, which I'll touch on later.

I had finally relieved the pressure of the balloon payment and the negative cash flow of the six-plex. It was a relatively smooth transition and we closed within one month.

How I Got a Banker to Give Me a House Plus $3,000 Cash

In the interim before the six-plex closed, a fellow from my real estate office approached me one day with some interesting information. I had mentioned to him that I bought and rennovated houses in New York at one time. He asked me if I still did this, and I told him that I did, when I could find one.

He told me of a lady who owned a home in Cape Coral that was being foreclosed. It had been vacant for a year or so, since her husband had left her. The lady had horrible memories in the house and had moved out a year earlier. Her son had moved in with some friends and a pack of dogs and cats. They had made the payments for a while, but had since moved out. We went and looked at it that same day.

The place was in a horrible state. There was animal excrement on every bit of carpeting, garbage strewn about, and the lawn was out of control. As a matter of fact, it was perfect! All the signs of a good deal were there. I was ready to meet the lady who owned it.

Steve had known Barbara (the owner) for several years. When we arrived, she told us her story. Apparently, she had bought the house (which was only 9 years old) new and her parents had lent her the $14,000 down payment. She owed $22,000 on the mortgage, which a local savings and loan carried. They were about six months into foreclosing, so it wouldn't be long before she lost her entire interest on the property. There were other complications, too. Her ex-husband's name was also on the deed. She had placed the house in the hands of the court and they appointed a Court Master to act in good faith for her. Transfer of title would be through what is called a masters deed.

Barbara was only interested in recouping the $14,000 that her parents had lent her to buy the house. She didn't care how it was paid, either. I made her the following offer. I would have the savings and loan either give me a new mortgage, or I would assume the old one of $22,000. I would pay Barbara the $14,000 in the form of a second mortgage over 20 years at 11% . However, there would be no payments, interest or principal, for two years, and no interest would accrue over that period of time.

Barbara accepted the offer. Now, the court had to accept it. I wrote a letter to the Court Master and to the judge with my offer enclosed.

Then, I went to the savings and loan to see what they would do to help. I had several things in my favor on this deal. First of all, it would save the bank money if they sold the house before foreclosure. Secondly, the house was in such a state that the bank would have to sink about $10,000 into it before they could even start to market it. With the real estate market so slow they would probably have to sit on the place for quite a while.

After several sit-down negotiations, the branch manager and I made a deal. He would give me a new $30,000 mortgage. With the proceeds I would satisfy the old $22,000 mortgage, and I would pay $5,000 toward the legal fees and costs they had incurred. After that, the house would be mine.

Oh yes, I almost forgot! But you caught it, didn't you? If the bank gave me a $30,000 mortgage and only $27,000 of it went to expenses, what happened to the other $3,000?

I hope you guessed it. At the closing when I took title to the house, the bank wrote me a check for $3,000. The branch manager and I agreed that I would need some money to get the house back in shape. Finally, I was getting back on track.

We did use the monies for improvements. We re carpeted the entire house, repainted it from top to bottom, and rented a chipper and dump truck to clear away the debris.

As a matter of fact, Ingrid and I now live in the house! It has three bedrooms, two baths, a Florida room, a private 10'x18' office for me, and a lovely yard. The house appraises for about $63. That gave me a ready made equity of $19,000 the day I moved in. This deal was a shot in the arm for me. Now I had two bank mortgages in Florida totaling $172,000. This would surely help establish my credibility with other lending institutions.

I closed on that property in December. Also in December, I finally closed on my last four buildings in New York. The cash proceeds were approximately $10,000. As I told you, I sold those out for a low down payment, but would get a very nice mortgage payment over the next ten years.

With the closing proceeds, I paid off some short term debts which had accumulated. The balance was put into my account for other real estate investments.

On the following pages are the actual agreements and copies of the bank's checks to me.

Russell + Ingrid Whitney
343 Cape Coral Pkwy
Cape Coral, Fla 33904

PURCHASE AND SALE AGREEMENT 8/29/82

The property that the buyers are agreeing to buy and the seller is agreeing to sell is commonly known as, 2520 S.E. 8th Place, in the city of Cape Coral and the county of Lee.

The buyers understand that the court master is Greg Burns, who has the seller's best interest in a fair offering on the property. The buyers also have been informed by Mr. Burns that the property is presently subject to forclosure proceedings by Coast Federal Bank.

The buyers wish to expediate a closing as soon as possible to avoid the seller losing a total interest in the property, as does the seller.

This offer is completely acceptable to Barbara Peplinski, the owner of said property. Miss Peplinski states that she is of sound mind, and is capable of determining a fair and acceptable offering on her property.

The terms and conditions hereunder are and have been agreeable to both the buying and selling parties. We submit these for the approval of the court. Furthermore we ask that the court help in expediting this matter to avoid undue hardship to Barbara Peplinski under the proceeding of forclosure.

TERMS AND CONDITIONS OF SALE - 2520 S.E. 8th Place, Cape Coral, Fla.

1. Buyer to assume present mortgage of approximately 21,000.00 at 12½%, or negotiate an acceptable mortgage with the present mortgage holder. (any renegotiation is for the sole purpose of improving the property.)

2. $14,000.00 to be paid to seller in full within two years from the date of closing. If buyer elects, they may, at the end of two years, pay the 14,000.00 under the following terms.

A. A 14,000.00 second mortgage note to the seller at the current rate of interest being charged by the first mortgage holder. However the interest rate will not exceed 12½%. The mortgage will be amortized over a 20 year period.

3. The buyers will pay for the expenses of the closing, including back taxes, back mortgage payments, court fees. The amount of the fees have been approximated at $2,000.00. Title insurance will also be payed by the buyers.

Russell H. Whitney
BUYER

Charles K Kuechelmann
WITNESS

Ingrid E. Whitney
BUYER

Barbara E. Peplinski
SELLER

DP-1059

SPECIAL MASTER'S DEED

BY THIS DEED, Gregory N. Burns, hereinafter called Grantor, who having been appointed Special Master for the sale of the real property described in this deed and such appointment being contained in that certain Final Judgment dated June 21, 1982, and recorded in Official Records Book 1614, Page 836, and the sale of the property described herein having been approved by Court Order of October 21, 1982, and recorded in Official Records Book 1651, Page 4271, in consideration of $10.00 paid by, Russell A. and Ingrid E. Whitney, (husband and wife) whose Post Office address is 2520 SE. 8th Place, Cape Coral, Florida 33904, hereinafter called Grantee, conveys to Grantee the following real property in Lee County, Florida:

> Lots 10 and 11, Block 820, Unit 21, Cape Coral Subdivision, according to the plat thereof, as recorded *in the Public Records of Lee County, Florida. *Plat Book 13, Pages 149 to 173, inclusive,

GRANTOR CONVENANTS with Grantee that Grantor has good right and lawful authority to sell and convey the property and Grantor warrants the title to the property for any acts of Grantor and will defend the title against the lawful claims of all persons claiming, by through or under Grantor.

Dated December 20, 1982.

Executed in the presence of:

Julie Fite

Gregory N. Burns
Special Master

STATE OF FLORIDA

COUNTY OF LEE

Before me this day personally appeared Gregory N. Burns who, after being duly sworn, says that he is the Special Master in this action and has read the foregoing, and its statements and contents are true.

Sworn to before me on December 20, 1982.

Notary Public

My Commission Expires:

NOTARY PUBLIC STATE OF FLORIDA AT LARGE
MY COMMISSION EXPIRES SEPT [illegible]
BONDED THRU GENERAL INS. UNDERWRITERS

Prepared by: Gregory N. Burns
P.O. Box 2194
Fort Myers, Florida
(813) 334-7107

Without Title Examination

PLEASE RETURN INSTRUMENT TO:
Chicago Title Insurance Agency
Cape Coral, Florida 33904

AFFIDAVIT

DP-1059

STATE OF FLORIDA)
: SS.
COUNTY OF LEE)

RUSSELL A. WHITNEY and INGRID E. WHITNEY, husband and wife

being first duly sworn upon oath, deposes and states:

1. That (I) and/or (We) the owner(s) of that certain real estate described as follows:

   Lots 10 and 11, Block 820, Unit 21, CAPE CORAL SUBDIVISION, according to the plat thereof as recorded in Plat Book 13, Pages 149 to 173, inclusive, in the Public Records of Lee County, Florida.

and more particularly described in a certain mortgage given by

RUSSELL A. WHITNEY and INGRID E. WHITNEY, husband and wife to

COAST FEDERAL SAVINGS AND LOAN ASSOCIATION for

$ 30,000.00 , dated at closing , which mortgage shall constitute a valid first lien upon said real estate when recorded in the Public Records of Lee County, Florida.

2. That (I) and/or (We) are in full, complete and undisputed possession of the above described property and that there are no leases, options, claims or interest held thereon by any other party except: If there are none, indicate by writing the word "NONE".

3. That there are no mechanics liens against said property and that there are no unpaid bills or claims outstanding for labor or material incident to the construction, repairing, renovating or improving of the buildings and improvements located upon said property; that no cautionary notices of any kind have been served with respect to labor performed or materials furnished upon said property except as follows: If there are none, indicate by writing the word "NONE".

4. That no judgment or decree has been entered in any court or any lien filed in this state or the United States against said affiants and which remains unsatisfied except as follows: If there are none, indicate by writing the word "NONE".

5. That this affidavit is made for the purpose of inducing CHICAGO TITLE INSURANCE AGENCY OF LEE COUNTY, INC. to insure the validity and priority of the lien of the above described mortgage.

PERSONALLY APPEARED and SWORN TO and SUBSCRIBED before me this

______ day of ______________, 19 ____

(NOTARY SEAL)

____
Notary Public State of Florida at Large

____

By RUSSELL A. WHITNEY

____

By INGRID E. WHITNEY

Mortgage Note, Fla. (Principal Payable in Monthly Installments - Interest Included) Form 37

Mortgage Note

$ 14,000.00 Cape Coral, Florida December 31st 1982

FOR VALUE RECEIVED the undersigned promises to pay to the order of

BARBARA E. KNICKERBOCKER

the principal sum of FOURTEEN THOUSAND DOLLARS AND NO/100 ($14,000.00) ------------------ Dollars

together with interest thereon at the rate of ** per cent per annum from December 31st, 1982 until maturity, both principal and interest being payable in Lawful Money of the United States, such principal sum and interest payable in installments as follows:

The sum of $14,000.00 (no interest is charged during the first 24 months of this note) shall become due and payable December 31st, 1984; at which time the Mortgagors may elect to pay this sum of $14,000.00 in 240 monthly installments which are to include interest, the first payment due January 31, 1985, and continuing until the entire principal and interest is paid in full. The interest rate charged shall be the same as the first mortgage holder, however, this rate shall not exceed 12 1/2% per annum. Prepayment may be made at anytime without penalty.

Such installment payments shall be applied first to the interest accruing under the terms of this note and then to a reduction of the principal indebtedness.

The makers and endorsers of this note further agree to waive demand, notice of non-payment and protest, and in the event suit shall be brought for the collection hereof, or the same has to be collected upon demand of an attorney, to pay reasonable attorney's fees for making such collection. All payments hereunder shall bear interest at the rate of ** percent per annum from maturity until paid. This note is secured by a mortgage of even date herewith and is to be construed and enforced according to the laws of the State of Florida; upon default in the payment of principal and/or interest when due, the whole sum of principal and interest remaining unpaid shall, at the option of the holders, become immediately due and payable. Failure to exercise this option shall not constitute a waiver of the right to exercise the same in the event of subsequent default.

Payable at 3822 SE. 11th Place, #103
Cape Coral, Florida 33904

or such other place as shall be designated by the holder of this note in writing.

** INTEREST RATE IS TO BE DETERMINED TWO YEARS FROM THE DATE OF THIS NOTE.

(SEAL)
RUSSELL A. WHITNEY (SEAL)
(SEAL)
INGRID E. WHITNEY (SEAL)

PLEASE DETACH AND RETAIN FOR YOUR RECORDS. No. 0 1505341

DATE	ACCOUNT NUMBER	DESCRIPTION	AMOUNT
12-31-82	150128418	LP ***Russell A. & Ingrid E. Whitney**	**$8801.19***

COAST FEDERAL SAVINGS
AND LOAN ASSOCIATION
Box 2199
Sarasota Florida 33678

DETACH AND RETAIN THIS STATEMENT
THE ATTACHED CHECK IS IN PAYMENT OF ITEMS DESCRIBED BELOW
IF NOT CORRECT PLEASE NOTIFY US PROMPTLY NO RECEIPT DESIRED

CHICAGO TITLE INSURANCE AGENCY OF LEE COUNTY, INC. - ESCROW ACCOUNT

DATE	ACCOUNT	DESCRIPTION	AMOUNT
12/30/82	DP-1059	Overage due back to Purchasers (NOTE: This amount is the out-of-pocket expenses due Coast Federal from Mr./Mrs. Whitney) (Recording Fees: $25.00) (Credit Report: $46.56) (Doc Stamps: $45.00) (1-Day Interest: $ 9.38) (Int Tax: $60.00) RE: Lots 10 & 11, Block 820, Unit 21, CAPE CORAL Peplinski to Whitney	$185.94

DETACH AND RETAIN THIS STATEMENT
THE ATTACHED CHECK IS IN PAYMENT OF ITEMS DESCRIBED BELOW
IF NOT CORRECT PLEASE NOTIFY US PROMPTLY NO RECEIPT DESIRED

CHICAGO TITLE INSURANCE AGENCY OF LEE COUNTY, INC. - ESCROW ACCOUNT

DATE	ACCOUNT	DESCRIPTION	AMOUNT
12/30/82	DP-1059	Overage due back to Purchasers RE: Lots 10 & 11, Block 820, Unit 21, CAPE CORAL Peplinski to Whitney	$2,673.41

Why Do Only A Select Few Make It Big?

I started gearing up now for a new surge. I finally felt as if I were getting back on track. I had some cash in the bank, and my credibility with them was gaining ground.

I was disgusted. That's right, disgusted! Disgusted with losing so much time. My initial goals were to have a net worth of a million dollars by the time I was 26 years old.

There was no reason for me to miss that goal, except that I had lost time by getting off track. Happy I am indeed to have the knowledge of what disgust really means. Recognizing disgust in your attitude is one of the first signs of getting back on track. Disgust, you will remember, is the first ingredient to start a day of turn-around in your life. The next step was making the decision to change; a strong decision—a commitment.

My decision included several things. First of all I needed to forget the peripheral stuff. By that, I mean all of the things that had side-tracked me and made me lose sight of my goals. I had to make the decision and commitment to ignore everything else and go to work strictly on real estate investing. I had to do all the things I did in my first year to create the deals and generate the money to expand.

The next step was to attend some seminars and get some updated reading material on current trends in the market. The world of finance is changing all the time. It's not less lucrative—not at all. There are just always new and different techniques to deal in the changing market. I will explain some of the newest of these in detail toward the book's end.

Let me show you what disgust and decision can do to a person's life. In January, 1983, I attended a real estate seminar to shake some life back into me. The seminar was organized around a variety of speakers. Six or seven speakers in separate conference rooms were speaking at the same time. You could choose the area of investing you wanted to learn about.

Several of the speakers were really inspiring! It was a four-day seminar and by the second day I wanted to leave so that I could go home and get to work. I had learned some new techniques and gotten a refresher on many that I had just forgotten or stopped using. I also met some outstanding people and made some good contacts. Seminars are wonderful places for making nationwide contacts, for finding investmentsand investors. On the last day of the seminar, I planned my course of action.

First, I started running my ad in the local newspaper. This ad, which I'll give you at the end of the book, has always worked well for me. It gets the phone ringing with people asking me to buy their properties. Next, I scanned the Multiple Listing Service looking for deals. I had 1,000 business cards printed which I placed on houses and gave out freely.

I then formed a partnership with Dan Kelly, the fellow who moved from New York with me. At this time, he had been working for a Realty company as an associate. He was doing all right, but he knew that the job was a dead-end proposition. There is no money in selling for a commission. The big money is in buying and selling for yourself.

I came home so excited and full of energy that it even regenerated Dan. We both decided on a vigorous course of action to achieve some ambitious goals. Within the next three weeks, we purchased well over $500,000 worth of property with no money of our own! The local newspaper did a story on us and we ended up forming an association of various public officials and politicians to lobby Washington, DC. for federal rehab money. To date, it looks as if we may get three quarters of a million dollars allocated for several projects. We formed a management and development company to manage our own properties. We also manage other peoples' properties for a nominal percentage.

It is very important to concentrate on maintaining a positive cash flow, especially in the initial stages of your investing career. Managing properties is an excellent source of income. It also keeps you in close touch with the owners of the properties. If you're doing a good job of managing, if they want to sell, you have a very good chance of getting a low or no money down deal from them.

Let me describe the details of our purchases in February. It was my intention in this book to describe the details all of my purchases. I feel that if you're involved in the purchases I made, through this book, it will be much more effective in helping you obtain your goals than just listing the steps.

I also included copies of many of the corresponding documents at the end of each chapter for your perusal. The deals are real and can be done by anyone that is willing to spend some time and look for them.

Many "How To Get Rich" books are written about real estate. Most of them tell you how to make a million dollars in seven minutes with no money down, no work, no risk and without getting out of bed. I'm being somewhat facetious, but it's just to drive the point home. When these books speak of "no money down", it doesn't necessarily mean no down payment. It could mean the money was borrowed elsewhere and applied to the down payment on the purchase. In my entire career, I have only made four actual no money down deals. Two of those deals were made in the three weeks that I'm about to describe to you.

I will give you the necessary tools to simplify the course of action for a beginning investor. I will tell you how to get the money, where to go for it, and what to say to get it. If you act, you win. It's that simple.

Chapter IV

Fundamental Laws (‘How To’ In Detail)

How to Make a No Money Down Offer Word for Word

I started getting some calls on the ad I put in the newspaper. A man called and told me he had two nine-year old duplexes in Fort Myers. They were concrete block, stucco construction, with central heat and air, appliances, and carpeting. They sounded good, and were located in an excellent part of town for rentals. I was also aware that duplexes in that area sold for $50,000 to $69,000.

When the owner told me that he just had two tenants evicted, owned three businesses and was looking for $41,000 for each duplex, I thought I might have something. We chatted for awhile, and I told him I would go look at them and call him back. Upon my inspection, I was quite impressed. With a little paint and fixing up, these would easily appraise for $55,000 apiece. The owner was only looking for $41,000.

I called him the following day and told him that Dan and I had an offer for him. We arranged to meet at his house on Saturday morning. I wrote the offer for $38,000 on each duplex, for a total of $76,000. The terms were: we would take his assumable 8% mortgage of $32,000, he would hold a second mortgage of $44,000 at 11% for 20 years, and no balloon.

Saturday morning, Dan and I arrived at the owner's home in Cape Coral. He invited us in and we sat and chatted for quite awhile. This is a technique that I have mentioned several times in recounting some of my deals. You must take time to talk to the seller about his home, his car, his business, his lovely pool, his kids, his grandchildren, his hobbies, or his wife's hobbies. You don't want to just plow into the offer.

Talk to the seller about what he wants to talk about. I guarantee if you discover what his interests are, he will carry the conversation for as long as you let him. People love to talk about themselves. Look around the room you're in (even if it's his office) and be observant. Are there any trophies on the shelves, plaques on the walls, pictures of children or grandchildren? If there are, why do you think he has them on the wall, or right out there where everyone can see them? He's proud of them, that's why! Do you think that if you ask, he'll tell you the story behind them? You bet.

When you show a lively interest in what they are interested in, do you know what you have done? Psychologically, you have obliged them to listen to you and your story with the same consideration. You have also built rapport by putting them at ease with your genuine interest. You'll know when it's time to present the offer because they'll ask you about it. I will usually engage them in conversation by asking them questions about themselves and letting them do most of the talking. After a time, they actually feel a little guilty about taking up so much time with their stories. That's when out comes my offer, along with a little presentation.

In the case of this owner, here's what happened. I noticed about eight bowling trophies on a shelf in the living room where we were sitting. I simply asked who the bowler was in the house. The owner's wife perked right up and smiled. She didn't say much more, so I asked what her average was. That was all the encouragement she needed! She told me about the Thursday league and how Madge Williams drinks too much, how she does better in the Tuesday league and a whole array of bowling stories. Boy, did I touch a hot button. We then talked about the owner's solar business, about the tenants he just had evicted, and about his car wash in Michigan that he had sold ten years ago and now had to foreclose on.

Are you getting the drift here? It is essential to built rapport and make the seller like you. If he likes you and trusts you, he's definitely more apt to help you. Let's get back to the Carters. We offered them $76,000 for their two duplexes. We would assume $32,000 in mortgages and they would hold $44,000 in a second at 11% for 20 years, fixed. No money down! We wrote in the contract that we would pay the closing costs. I thought that was very sporting of us.

When we got to the presentation, here's how it went. I said, "We are buying a lot of property. I have been doing this for many years and now own quite a bit. I brought you over some pictures of my properties so you can see how well I keep them maintained." This is the main concern with most sellers when we ask them to hold a mortgage for us.

"Would that concern you?" I asked. (Note: he has to say yes. The question doesn't allow for a no.) "You mentioned on the phone that you had another business and several other investments, didn't you?" I continued. "I thought that you would probably rather hold some of the mortgage, instead of getting a large down payment because of the tax consequences. Would you have to pay a pretty good size gain tax if we gave you all cash?" (Yes, again.) "We really couldn't pay all cash but I'm glad that I was able to foresee some of the things you would run into when you do sell the properties." (I show empathy and concern for him, too—not just gimmee, gimmee, gimmee.)

"To be perfectly honest, even if we put $5,000 down on all of the property we're buying, it wouldn't be long before we'd run out of money. Since this is our full time business, we have to structure the offers this way. If you'll notice, we did try to structure it so you would come out better too! Do you see why?" (Of course he says no.) "Well, the $44,000 that we owe you will be paid off at $463 each and every month for the next 20 years.

"That second mortgage would have a value, if you total those payments, of $111,120 plus the $32,000 we are assuming. Therefore, you will realize $143,120. So, you see, there are some definite advantages to selling this way. The first would be for tax reasons. The second would be much more money to you over time, as though you were the bank. The third reason is, you relieve yourself of the headache of managing the property. We, of course, will use our monies to fix them up, paint them and get some landscaping done right away."

NOW READ THE FOLLOWING CAREFULLY!

At this point in the presentation, after the rapport has been built, you've established some credibility with pictures of properties you owned (before-and-afters are great for this) and you've presented some logical reasons why they should consider this offer. The most important thing to do now is SHUT UP and not say another word until the seller comments! Look back to the dialogue and note where I stopped talking. It's like a tennis game where I have hit the ball into the opponent's court. There is nothing I can possibly do or accomplish until the ball is hit back to me. Silence does not constitute a return of the ball.

In this case, the owner remained silent for about 30 seconds. Do you know how long that is? Most people would have felt uncomfortable and would have started jabbering away. In this case, as in many others, it probably would have killed the deal. Dan and I sat without saying a word. When the silence broke, the owner said, "Well, can we change this interest rate from 11% to 11-1/2%?" Again, learn a lesson here. The average person would say, "Oh sure, that won't be a problem at all. Here, I'll do it right now and we can all sign."

Instead, Dan and I looked directly at each other, trying desperately not to smile or jump out of our chairs in elation. Dan said, "Well, I don't know. We didn't figure the numbers that way." He pulled out his amortization book, punched some numbers into his calculator (who knows whether or not he even turned the calculator on) and said, "Russ, I think it will be okay. What do you think?" I said, "As long as there is a little left over to cover the necessary maintenance, it will be fine."

"Wait a minute," said the owner. I almost swallowed my heart. "I'll do it this way," he said, "but I want a closing as soon as possible. I want it next week before I leave for Michigan." We had to scramble with the assumption papers from the bank and the title company, but we did it in one week!

The day we were to close on this property, I was discussing the terms and price to a Realtor in Fort Myers. Actually, I was picking up a signed contract on another property we had purchased. He offered me $10,000 cash that day to assign him the contract for those two duplexes! In one week, just for finding that deal we could pocket $10,000 in cash, no questions asked.

Did we do it? No, and I'll tell you why. The owner owned four more income properties in Fort Myers. He wanted to sell those, too, and told us that after he gets his payments on time for a few months we could make a deal on the rest of the properties. If we had sold them to make a quick $10,000 profit, he would feel we took advantage of him. Chances are we wouldn't get the rest of the properties.

That reasoning may not prevail in another similar situation, though. Would we take the $10,000 if the duplexes were his only properties? Probably not, and, again, I'll explain why. When we examine the circumstances, we find several things.

First of all, the monthly cash flow is $1,200. The mortgage payments are $771, leaving a balance of $429. If we deduct our only other expenses, taxes and insurance, of $120 per month, we have a net positive cash flow of $309 per month.

Taking the quick $10,000 means a clean profit, but there is a short term capital gain[1] to consider. Here's what we did do. We applied for a $15,000 home improvement loan. The payment was $297 per month, leaving a small positive cash flow. The $15,000 coming from a loan is not taxable as ordinary income, so we got to keep it all. We also added another asset to our financial statement which will increase our net worth. Market value of the duplexes is approximately $55,000 apiece, which leaves us with a total of $110,000, less the mortgage and home improvement loan covering the property. The loans total $91,000, giving us an equity of $19,000 which we also add to our net worth. We also add $15,000, free and clear, to our bank account.

If we want to take it a step further, we could now sell the property with a low down payment of $5,000 and have the buyer purchase subject to the first mortgage, second mortgage, and the home improvement loan. To top it off, we could grab another $5,000. This game of real estate investing can sure be fun!

The duplexes turned out to be a super buy. At the closing, our costs totalled $1,310. This was for the "assumption of mortgage" fee ($250 for each duplex), recording fees, and title insurance. We agreed to pay the closing costs, so actually it wasn't a "zero" down payment. However, the $1,310 is part of a $5,000 home improvement loan, so it is zero down.

Another pleasant part of the closing was the $500 check the owner wrote to us for the security deposits, plus his return of our $100 earnest money. So, deducting those, we closed $110,000 worth of property with $800 of borrowed money one week after meeting the seller.

Earlier in this book, I mentioned something about the Doubting Thomases of the world. My statement was to the effect that I had bought properties in 1978 and 1979 when interest rates were low and the market was better. How many people (the negative thinkers) said that it couldn't be done that way anymore? I said I would prove to you that this way of thinking is wrong.

Well, this closing took place on February 23, 1983. One year later I bought a $200,000 six-plex with only $6,000 of my money. Eleven months had passed since I purchased the seven-plex for $75,000 with only $4,700 down. All of these were purchased in 1982 and 1983. Things are still good. It all depends on how you choose to see things. If you think you'll lose, you will. If you think you're a winner, I'll be the first to congratulate you!

On the following page is the signed offer we presented the owner with the closing statement and assumption papers.

SALES CONTRACT

Cape Coral, Florida FEBRUARY 13, 1983

Receipt is hereby acknowledged by the undersigned broker of the sum of:

ONE HUNDRED DOLLARS AND NO/100 (TO BE APPLIED TO CLOSING COSTS) Dollars ($ 100.00

from RUSSELL WHITNEY AND DAN KELLY

as a deposit on account of the purchase price of the following described property upon the terms and conditions as stated herein. Said deposit, and any further deposits received on this transaction to be held in Stoffijo & Haywood Realty, Inc. escrow account in compliance with Florida Real Estate law.

Description of Property, same being in LEE County, Florida. (SEE LEGAL DESCRIPTION ATTACHED)

IMPROVED PROPERTY LOCATED ON 5648-5652 NINTH AVE. FT. MYERS, FL. (TWO DUPLEXES)

Purchase Price: SEVENTY-SIX THOUSAND DOLLARS AND NO/100---------------- Dollars ($ 76,000.00

Terms and conditions of sale:

$76,000.00 - PURCHASE PRICE
36,000.00 - SUBJECT TO TWO $18,000.00 MORTGAGES (APPROXIMATE BALANCES)
40,000.00 - SELLER TO HOLD APPROXIMATELY $40,000.00 IN A SECOND MORTGAGE FOR 20 YEARS AT 11.5% INTEREST WITH MONTHLY PAYMENTS OF $426.57 INCLUDING PRINCIPAL AND INTEREST. NO PENALTY FOR PREPAYMENT. TOTAL PAYOUT WILL BE APPROXIMATELY $102,376.80.

NOTE: BUYERS AGREE TO PAY ALL CLOSING COSTS INCLUDING TITLE INSURANCE.

BUYERS ALSO AGREE TO IMMEDIATELY PLACE BETWEEN $4000.00 AND $5000.00 IN IMPROVEMENTS ON THE PROPERTY.

Buyers Agree to Accept Appliances And All Equipment As Is.

1. ACCEPTANCE: If this offer is not accepted by the seller on or before FEBRUARY 13, 1983, the aforesaid deposit monies shall be, at the option of the buyer, returned to him, and this agreement shall be null and void.
2. EVIDENCE OF TITLE: Seller shall furnish, at his expense, an up-to-date abstract XXXXXX, or apply $ XXXXX toward the total cost of title insurance. In the event title is not found to be good, marketable and insurable, all monies paid by the buyer shall be returned, and the parties hereto shall be released from all obligations; or, buyer may accept title as is.
3. CONVEYANCE: Seller shall convey the aforesaid property to the buyer by General Warranty Deed.
4. RESTRICTIONS AND EASEMENTS: It is understood and agreed that this property is being sold and purchased subject to the restrictions and limitations of record common to the neighborhood, and subject to any assessments for public utilities which may be of record. Furthermore, it is understood and agreed that this property is being sold and purchased subject to the approval of a percolation and soil analysis, if sanitary sewerage is not available to the property, at the seller's expense. Futhermore, seller must furnish on any building an affirmative test that no wood boring insects exist and there is no damage existing from previous infestations.
5. PRORATIONS: Insurance, interest, rents and other expenses or revenues of said property shall be prorated as of the date of closing. Taxes and other assessments shall be prorated as of the date of closing on the basis of the last assessment records available.
6. APPLIANCES: All electrical mechanical and gas appliances shall be in working condition at date of closing, normal wear and tear excepted.
7. CLOSING DATE: This transaction shall be closed and the buyer shall pay the balance of the monies and execute all papers necessary for the completion of his purchase on or before MARCH 1, 1983; otherwise, the deposit monies paid this date shall be retained by the seller or agent as liquidated and agreed damages, and the parties hereto shall be released from all obligations under this instrument.
8. POSSESSION will be given on or before AT CLOSING.
9. RISK: Until delivery of the deed, the risk of loss or damage to said property is assumed by the seller.
10. THIS contract shall be binding upon the parties hereto, their respective heirs, executors and assigns.
11. SELLER'S EXPENSES: Seller is to pay the following: (a) cost of furnishing complete Abstract of title certified to date (and also current chattel search if personal property is included as part of the above described property); (b) preparation of warranty deed and deed stamps; (c) mortgage intangible tax and recording fee for any purchase-money mortgage to seller; (d) real estate Brokerage fee; (e) special taxes or assessments for which a bill has been rendered, on or before the date of the acceptance of this contract; (f) condominium transfer fee, if any.
12. BUYER'S EXPENSES: Buyer is to pay for the following: (a) recording fee for warranty deed; (b) preparation of note and mortgage, and note stamps on note, for any purchase-money mortgage, or any costs of any institutional loan secured by Buyer; (c) mortgage transfer fee, if required; (d) cost of survey, if required; (e) recording of Approval for Membership, if applicable; (f) special taxes or assessment for which no bill has been rendered, on or before the date of the acceptance of this contract.
13. PRO-RATIONS: The following items will be pro-rated at closing, as of the closing date: (a) real estate taxes; (b) interest on any assumed indebtedness; (c) insurance, unless Buyer elects to take out new insurance; (d) rent; (e) condominium maintenance, if applicable.
14. ASSIGNABILITY: (check one) Buyer ☒ May assign ☐ May not assign, contract.

By DANIEL M. KELLY

I, or we, agree to purchase the above described property on the terms and conditions stated in the above instrument.

Witness:

Purchaser: [signature] Date: 2/17/83

_______________ ( ) [signature] (Seal)

_______________ ( ) [signature] (Seal)

I, or we, agree to sell the above described property to the above named purchaser on the terms and conditions stated in the above instrument.

Witness:

Seller: Date: 2/14/82

_______________ ( ) Robert S. Coates (Seal)

_______________ ( ) [signature] (Seal)

I, or we, agree to pay to the above signed broker, as commission for finding a purchaser for the above property, the sum of:

_______________ Dollars ($ _______)

or one half of the deposit in case same is forfeited by purchaser, provided the same shall not exceed the full amount of the commission.

Witness:

_______________ ( ) _______________ (Seal)

_______________ ( ) _______________ (Seal)

Executive Title Insurance Agency, Inc.

CLOSING STATEMENT FILE No. 2203

CLOSING DATE February 23, 1983

PURCHASERS: DANIEL [illegible]. KELLY & RUSSELL A. WHITNEY

IN RE Lots 21 & 22, Block 28, Unit 5, PINE MANOR SUBDIVISION

SELLERS ROBERT L. CARTER & BEVERLY J. CARTER, Husband and Wife

BROKER NONE

	DEBITS	CREDITS
PURCHASE PRICE	76,000.00	
Deposit To		
Surtax on Deed		
State Stamps on Deed	342.00	
Recording warranty deed	5.00	
recording two mortgages @ 13.00 each	26.00	
2 March payments @ $154.37 each	[illegible]	
TOTAL OF BOTH MORTGAGE ASSUMPTION BALANCES		$32,215.98
Mortgage PURCHASE MONEY MORTGAGE		21,717.60
Mortgage PURCHASE MONEY MORTGAGE		21,717.59
State Stamps Mgt Note two @ $32.70 each	65.40	
Intangible Tax on Mortgage two @ $43.44 each	86.88	
Mortgage Tranfer Fee two @ $250.00 each	500.00	
Abstract of Title		
Title Insurance Premium	[illegible].75	
Broker's Commission		
Hazard Insurance		
Prorate Interest: 2/2/83 to 2/23/83		80.64
Pro-Rations Interest 2/2/83 to 2/23/83		80.43
1983 Taxes based on 1982 rates of $1,269.10 for 54 days		187.76
Hazard Insurance		
Mortgage [illegible] amortization schedule	5.00	
Taxes Due: City and/or County		
TOTAL	77,~~[illegible]~~ 216.03	76,000.00
*DUE (~~To~~) (From) PURCHASER		1316.03
*DUE (To) (From) SELLER		
TOTAL	77,[illegible]	77,216.03

*It is expressly understood and agreed between the parties hereto, that when proration of taxes herein is based on the prior year's tax figures, Executive Title Insurance Agency is not responsible for the accuracy thereof. Differences, if any, shall be later adjusted between the purchaser and seller when current year's tax figures are available.

APPROVED DANIEL [illegible] KELLY

APPROVED RUSSELL A. WHITNEY

Florida Federal

TO: Bill Townsend, Executive Title Ins. Agency

FROM: Eunice Griswold, McGregor

DATE: February 21, 1983

SUBJECT: Loan #3-604380; Non-prequalified Assumtion
Carter to Kelly/Whitney

The following figures reflect monies due upon assumption of this loan:

Loan Transfer Fee $250.00

The following assumption figures apply:

Principal balance	$16,109.74
Interest Rate	8.00
Contractual Payment	154.37
Payment Due:	March 1, 1983
Per diem	3.83

INTEREST IS CHARGED IN ARREARS

Below is a list of all documents and transfer fees due to complete subject transfer:

1. Transfer fee of $250.00
2. Anti-coercion, signed by borrowers
3. Copy of executed deed (recording information required when received)
4. Mortgage Loan Transfer (completed in all areas where indicated in yellow) attached.
5. Completed insurance memorandums in new owners names.

Upon receipt of these items our records will be changed to reflect the new ownership.

Sincerely,

Eunice Griswold
Assistant Branch Manager

TO: Bill Townsend, Executive Title Ins. Agency

FROM: Eunice Griswold, McGregor

DATE: February 21, 1983

SUBJECT: Loan #3-604381; Non-prequalified Assumption
Carter to Kelly/Whitney
Closing date of 2/23/83

The following figures reflect monies due upon assumption of this loan:

Loan Transfer Fee	$250.00

The following assumptions figures apply:

Principal balance	$16,106.34
Interest rate	8.00
Contractual Payment	154.37
Payment Due:	March 1, 1983
Per diem	3.84

INTEREST IS CHARGED IN ARREARS

Below is a list of all documents and transfer fees due to complete subject transfer:

1. Transfer fee of $250.00
2. Anti-coercion signed by borrowers
3. Copy of executed deed (recording information required when received)
4. Mortgage Loan Transfer (completed in all areas where indicated in yellow) attached.
5. Completed insurance memorandums in new owners names.

Upon receipt of these items our records will be changed to reflect the new ownership.

Sincerely,

Eunice Griswold
Assistant Branch Manager

Beware of Balloons! Negotiate with Your Banker

Let me explain how we found our sources of funding. We knew we were going to be needing fix-up money and more seed capital for investments. We started making appointments with different bankers to find out if they had short term money to lend for home improvements, until we could secure long term money.

The response was pretty favorable. They all seemed to have money, and all seemed anxious to lend it. However, bankers and other lenders are very cautious.

Currently, the rate of foreclosures is higher than any other time in our nation's history. Banks are being very cautious with interest rates. None of the institutions want to get locked into low, fixed rates again.

There are many variations in lending policies with banking institutions. Be very careful to understand the type of loan presented before you sign. I am naturally leery of any type of balloon payment. If a lender wants a three or five year callable (balloon) mortgage, try to negotiate a re-negotiable rate instead.

This simply means they may raise the interest rate to the then current rate, but may not call in the mortgage in full. Many people are intimidated by their bankers into accepting balloon mortgages, especially if they're new to investing. They may take this type of financing out of desperation, just to get something going.

They may also feel that they are projecting an image of being unsophisticated or financially incapable of dealing with these terms if they don't accept it.

That is simply not true! You can have a natural, conservative and verbal offensive prepared when your banker presents you with those terms. Let's pretend that I'm in the office of a big, intimidating banker and I'm applying for a loan. Watch how I turn the situation to my advantage.

"Well, Mr. Whitney, we'd be happy to lend you 80% of the appraised value of the property. We can give you a 12-1/2% loan for 25 years with a three year balloon payment."

"Excuse me, did you say a three year balloon?"

"Yes, Mr. Whitney, we have a three year or a five year."

"I see. Well, I'll be perfectly honest with you. I've been in this business for some time now and I've seen these balloon arrangements cripple people. You would be asking me to make a promise I may not be able to keep. I have an impeccable credit rating and my business would be absolutely destroyed if I didn't take precautions. Would you agree, Mr. Banker?" (Of course he says yes, but he's curious to see what I'm getting at.) I continue. "Mr. Banker, if you make that a re-negotiable rate mortgage I would feel much safer doing business with you. By that I mean, if my payments are timely, my taxes paid and our agreement upheld on my end, I would think the bank could make some type of written commitment to me to re-negotiate, rather than call in the mortgage." You will be surprised at how flexible the banks really are.

What we have just discussed is a very strong argument for the borrower. You will have your banker's respect because of your keen foresight and conservatism. If he won't give you a commitment and insists on a balloon, you should go down the street to the next institution. When you get there, tell them why you're there! Tell them about the crazy man up the street who wants you to make a promise you might not be able to keep! Also, before you spend a lot of time there, make sure *they* are not as crazy as the first bank.

The following pages contain some information on an adjustable mortgage loan.

IMPORTANT INFORMATION ABOUT THE ADJUSTABLE MORTGAGE LOAN
PLEASE READ CAREFULLY

You have received an application form for an adjustable mortgage loan ("AML"). The AML differs from other mortgages with which you may be familiar.

General Description of Adjustable Mortgage Loan

The adjustable mortgage loan is a flexible loan instrument. Its interest rate may be adjusted by the lender from time to time. Such adjustments will result in increases or decreases in your payment amount, in the outstanding principal loan balance, in the loan term, or in all three (see discussion below relating to these types of adjustments). Federal regulations place no limit on the amount by which interest rate may be adjusted either at any one time or over the life of the loan, or on the frequency with which it may be adjusted. Adjustment to the interest rate must reflect the movement of a single, specified index (see discussion below). This does not mean that the particular loan agreement you sign must, by law, permit unlimited interest rate changes. It merely means that, if you desire to have certain rate adjustment limitations placed in your loan agreement, that is a matter you should negotiate with the lender. You may also want to make inquiries concerning the loan terms offered by other lenders on AML's to compare the terms and conditions.

Another flexible feature of the AML is that the regular payment amount may be increased or decreased by the lender from time to time to reflect changes in the interest rate. Again, Federal regulations place no limitations on the amount by which the lender may adjust payments at any one time, or on the frequency of payment adjustments. If you wish to have particular provisions in your loan agreement regarding adjustments to the payment amount, you should negotiate such terms with the lender.

A third flexible feature of the AML is that the outstanding principal loan balance (the total amount you owe) may be increased or decreased from time to time when, because of adjustments to the interest rate, the payment amount is either too small to cover interest due on the loan, or larger than is necessary to pay off the loan over the remaining term of the loan.

The final flexible feature of the AML is that the loan term may be lengthened or shortened from time to time, corresponding to an increase or decrease in the interest rate. When the term is extended in connection with a rate increase, the payment amount does not have to be increased to the same extent as if the term had not been lengthened. In no case may the total term of the loan exceed 40 years.

The combination of these four basic features allows an association to offer a variety of mortgage loans. For example, one type of loan could permit rate adjustments with corresponding changes in the payment amount. Alternatively, a loan could permit rate adjustments to occur more frequently than payment adjustments, limit the amount by which the payment could be adjusted, and/or provide for corresponding adjustments to the principal loan balance.

Index

Adjustments to the interest rate of an AML must correspond directly to the movement of an index, subject to such rate-adjustment limitations as may be contained in the loan contract. If the index has moved down, the lender must reduce the interest rate by at least the decrease in the index. If the index has moved up, the lender has the right to increase the interest rate by that amount. Although taking such an increase is optional by the lender, you should be aware that the lender has this right and may become contractually obligated to exercise it.

> The index to be used for your AML will be the national average mortgage contract rate for major lenders on the purchase pf previously occupied homes. This index is computed monthly by the Federal Home Loan Bank Board in Washington, D.C. and is published monthly in the Board's FHLBB Journal. The initial index value for your loan will be set on the date the loan closes (the date you sign the mortgage and note). For calendar year 1980, this index had a high value of 13.740% in May of 1980 and a low value of 11.780% occurring in January of 1980.

Key Terms of Coast Federal Savings and Loan Association's Adjustable Mortgage Loan

Following is a summary of the basic terms on the type of AML to be offered to you. This summary is intended for reference purposes only. Important information relating specifically to your loan will be contained in the loan agreement.

Index:	FHLBB National Average Contract Rate on Previously Occupied Homes
Initial Index Value:	Set at closing
Initial Contract Interest Rate:	Set at time of loan commitment
Loan Term:	30 years
Frequency of Rate Adjustment:	Every 12 months from the change date of loan
Frequency of Payment Adjustment: (Exclusive of Escrow)	Every 12 months from the change date of loan
Maximum Rate Change at one time	None - No Cap
Maximum Rate Change over life of loan	None - No Cap
Adjustment to Principal Loan Balance	None - No Negative Amortization

M-181

How Your Adjustable Mortgage Loan Would Work

The initial interest rate offered by Coast Federal Savings and Loan Association on your AML will be established and disclosed to you at time of commitment, based on market conditions at the time.

The interest rate on your AML is subject to adjustment according to the movement of the index selected for your loan. Changes in the interest rate on your loan will be determined at 12 month intervals from the change date of your loan. The interest rate on your loan will adjust up or down depending on whether the index at that time has increased above or decreased below the initial index value. The amount of change in the index will be added or subtracted to the initial contract rate at each interest rate adjustment period to determine the new rate on your AML. At an interval of 12 months from the change date of your loan, the payment on your AML may adjust to reflect interest rate changes that have occurred during the preceding initial period and each 12 months thereafter. In the event of interest rate increase or decrease the principal balance of your loan will not be adjusted to accommodate the full interest rate change permitted by the loan agreement. Annual review and adjustment of your principal and interest payments allows for continuous amortization of your loan balance. The original loan payment will remain fixed for the initial period, and each payment determined after the payment adjustment will also remain fixed for the next 12 succeeding months.

Notice of Payment Adjustments

Coast Federal Savings and Loan Association will send you notice of an adjustment to the payment amount at least 30 but not more than 45 days before it becomes effective. The notice will contain the following information:

1. The fact that the payment on your loan with the association, secured by a mortgage on your property as described in the loan agreement, is scheduled to be adjusted on a particular date;
2. That the outstanding balance of your loan on the payment adjustment date, assuming timely payment of the remaining payments due by that date;
3. The interest rate on your loan as of the adjustment date, the index value on which that rate is based, the period of time for which the interest rate will be in effect, the next following payment adjustment date, and the rate adjustment date between the upcoming payment adjustment date and the next scheduled payment adjustment date;
4. The payment amount as of the payment adjustment date;
5. The date on which the rate was adjusted since the last payment adjustment, the rates on each such rate adjustment date, and the index values corresponding to each such date;
6. The date on which the outstanding principal loan balance was adjusted since the last payment adjustment, and the net change in the outstanding principal loan balance since the last payment adjustment;
7. The fact that the borrower may prepay the entire loan or a part of it without penalty at any time;
8. The title and telephone number of an association employee who can answer questions about the notice.

Prepayment Penalty

You may prepay an AML in whole or in part without penalty at any time during the term of the loan.

Fees

You will be charged fees by Coast Federal Savings and Loan Association and by other persons in connection with the origination of your AML. The association will give you an estimate of these fees after receiving your loan application. However, you will not be charged any costs or fees in connection with any regularly-scheduled adjustment to the interest rate, the payment, the outstanding principal loan balance, or the loan term initiated by the lender.

AML/mp
Revised 4/82

An Example of How Your Adjustable Mortgage Loan Would Work

Below is an example of how your AML works showing 3 year rate and payment adjustments. The numbers and rates used in this example will probably be different than those in the actual loan if it is granted to you.

For your loan, there is an annual interest rate and payment adjustment. At payment adjustment, change is sufficient to re-establish the amortization schedule. There are no rate or payment change limitations. The FHLBB National Average Contract Rate on previously occupied homes is the index.

Example

The loan was closed August 30, 1981; the first month of the loan is September, 1981; and the first principal and interest payment is due October 1, 1981.

Loan Amount: $50,000.00
Term: 30 years
Contract Interest Rate: 15-1/2%
Initial payment: $652.26 (set at closing)
Initial Index Value: 14%
First Rate Adjustment: September, 1982 (assume new index value of 15%)
Date of First Payment Adjustment: September, 1982 (payable October 1, 1982)
Payment Adjustment Notice: Sent July 15, 1982

Month	Index Value	Index Change	Interest Rate	Payment	Payment Change	Balance
						$50,000.00
Sep 81	14.00%		15.50%	$652.26		49,993.57
Oct 81			15.50	652.26		49,987.06
Nov 81			15.50	652.26		49,980.47
Dec 81			15.50	652.26		49,973.79
Jan 82			15.50	652.26		49,967.02
Feb 82			15.50	652.26		49,960.17
Mar 82			15.50	652.26		49,953.23
Apr 82			15.50	652.26		49,946.20
May 82			15.50	652.26		49,939.08
Jun 82			15.50	652.26		49,931.87
Jul 82			15.50	652.26		49,924.56
Aug 82			15.50	652.26		49,917.16
Sep 82	15.00%	+1.00%	16.50%	$692.34	+ $40.08	49,911.18
Oct 82			16.50	692.34		49,905.12
Nov 82			16.50	692.34		49,898.98
Dec 82			16.50	692.34		49,892.75
Jan 83			16.50	692.34		49,886.44
Feb 83			16.50	692.34		49,880.04
Mar 83			16.50	692.34		49,873.55
Apr 83			16.50	692.34		49,866.97
May 83			16.50	692.34		49,860.30
Jun 83			16.50	692.34		49,853.54
Jul 83			16.50	692.34		49,846.69
Aug 83			16.50	692.34		49,839.74
Sep 83	13.50%	- .50%	15.00%	$632.74	- $19.52	49,830.00
Oct 83				632.74		

Interest Rate Adjustment

On the interest rate and payment adjustment date, the new interest rate on your loan will be equal to the original contract rate plus the difference between the initial index value and the index value most recently available as of the date of interest rate adjustment. The index value most recently available as of the date of notification of a payment adjustment when there is a scheduled payment adjustment. For example, we have assumed most recent index value for the September, 1982 rate adjustment is 15.00%. This is a plus 1.00% increase over the original index value of 14.00%. Therefore, the new interest rate in effect for this loan for September, 1982 to September, 1983 will be 16.50% (15.50 + 1.00) = 16.50% and a corresponding payment change September, 1982 to 692.34

Acknowledgement:
(I) (We) have received this date a copy of this AML form.

____

____

Date: ________________________

Coast Federal Savings

By: ________________________

How to Use Short Term Money

We researched our sources of financing. This is a constant part of investing. We established credit with several banks which would lend us $5,000 or more on a six-month interest only note. The interest costs about $50 per month. After the sixth month, the principal balance of $5,000 is due. You may pay this back in one of many ways. You can take a short term loan from another bank, pay that one off and extend it six more months. You might be able to just "roll the note" with the same bank. In other words, they will let you pay interest only for another six months.

The best way is to find a real estate investment that can be bought with $5,000 or less. Find one you can buy that will support a long term (ten or fifteen years) home improvement loan. Use the rent to cover both the mortgage and the home improvement loan. When you receive the loan, pay off the $5,000 short term note and put the other $5,000 in your pocket.

You can do it an even better way. Actually they're all good, but here's the way we did it with 4931 Orange Grove Boulevard. Again, this is during the first three weeks of February in our surge back into the market.

How and Why You Should Share the Wealth

A Realtor friend of mine came to me and told me of a *singular* listing his office had just acquired.

It was a three bedroom, one bath home in a $35,000 to $40,000 neighborhood. The owner lived in Pennsylvania and rented it to some less than desirable people. They had stopped paying the rent, which hampered his ability to make the $316 mortgage payments. We also learned that he had a mortgage at 18% with a finance company that was almost three months behind.

Now, all of that tells me a number of things. Especially, the 18% mortgage with a finance company.

I once had a banker tell me that banks are very wary of lending money to anyone who has a finance company"loan. This is because those people probably could not get a loan anywhere else. How true is it? I don't know, but I have never had to use one and wouldn't chance the after-effects. I felt this fellow could not get financing anywhere else and was probably hurting when he refinanced. Now, being behind a couple of months in payments, he would risk losing all of his investment in the property. Not only that, but his credit would be ruined.

I had my Realtor friend write an offer. We would buy the property "subject to,"[2] and make "payments on" the $15,500, 18% mortgage. We would pay the owner $4,500 within six months after the closing on the property. The seller would pay the real estate commission.

When I went to look at the house, I was amazed. It sits on a beautiful corner lot. With some interior and exterior paint, the house would appraise for about $38,000. The reason I knew its appraised value was two-fold. One, I've had experience buying, selling and looking at homes. Two, I had the house appraised. I have an appraiser who does work for several banks in the area. We pay him on every deal he appraises, after we fix-up, refinance, or take out a home improvement loan. He went out to the property and made me a list of things to repair. He said if these things were done, the house would appraise for $38,000. Now, we were armed and protected for our next move. The fix-up would cost about $2,000. We would refinance for 80% of the appraised value. Upon refinancing, after closing costs and points, we would gross about $29,000 of the $30,400 loan. $4500 would go to the seller leaving $24,500. $15,500 would pay off the 18% mortgage and $2,000 toward fixing it up. We would have $7,000 in tax free money until we paid the appraiser his fee of $500 and a fee of $500 to the person who brought the deal to my attention. So we would net $6,000 on the deal.

I know many investors who would not want to pay the appraiser or the person who put you into the deal to save the measly $1,000. Some people would say, "Yeah, $1,000 is nothing to a guy with bucks, like you. What about a little guy like me who's hurting for cash?" Remember, one of the reasons that attributes to one's success or failure is the way one thinks. When the appraiser gets his $500, who do you think will be on the top of the phone list when a deal comes around? As an appraiser, this man appraises foreclosures, repos, nice houses, old houses, and distressed houses. How many other appraisers or people in related fields does he know? I assure you, he will let other people know of "this guy" who pays $500 just to have him look at a house. In fact, if I had made more on the deal, I would have no qualms about giving him $1,000. The same holds true for the Realtor who brought the deal to my attention. They will "bird-dog" for you faithfully if you share the wealth. Let everybody make some money and you'll have no choice but to prosper.

That was deal number two in our first week of new birth. By the way, the $30,400 mortgage we secured on that house was an adjustable rate mortgage (ARM). This means that the interest rate will be adjusted yearly to whatever the agreement is. There is NO BALLOON.

Our payments on the mortgage were $297. Taxes and insurance totaled $60 per month. The rent is $400, leaving a net positive cash flow of $43 per month.

While doing the fix-up we put out a "for sale by owner" sign. We also advertised "$2,000 down, owner will carry." By using these tactics, we had a buyer within a few weeks. We sold for $38,000 with $2,000 down and wrapped $6,000 with the ARM mortgage. This also structured the sale so that the new buyers sent us the payment. We then sent the payment to the bank.

You see, I don't care for single family homes for long term investment in my portfolio. I prefer to utilize them as short term cash generators and turn them over for the monthly payment. For a $43 per month cash flow, I would rather help a couple get into a place with a little money down. Also, our payment on the wrap-around was more than $43, without any of the headaches. These are virtually guaranteed payments. If you do ten or twelve of those a year, you can certainly build up a nice little monthly income.

I like to have multi-units for longer term investments; duplexes, four-plexes, six-plexes, ten units, or even larger. They provide a much bigger cash flow and tax shelter than the single family homes.

If you are concerned about the short term capital gain tax because of selling the single families so quickly, let me explain. In my entire career of real estate investing, I have never paid any income taxes at all. If you consider the income averaging my accountant did the first big year of 1979, I haven't paid any income tax since 1976! I have zeroed out every year. Wait a minute! I promised you that this would be an accurate accounting of my investing career, didn't I? Then I must admit that last year, my accountant had me pay $28 at the end of the year. He said by paying a minimal amount, it lessens the percentages of an IRS computer kicking the return out for an audit. So, I have plenty of room for some short term turnovers and so will you.

My investment strategies are to get some cash flow on the multi-units needing repair. Put some up for sale, and keep some for the cash flow and shelter. Buy some prime units, like the six-plex on Cape Coral Parkway, for the appreciation, down the road, and the super tax shelter. I use the smaller units and single families on a wraparound to get a steady payment coming in. If you diversify into several areas, you cover yourself for any traumatic changes in the economy or your own personal life, for that matter.

The following page is a copy of the signed offer for 4931 Orange Grove.

2 See appendix.

Home Hunters Inc.

Joseph and Lucille Molina

of ______________________ (Ph __________) hereinafter called the Seller, and

Dan Kelly and or assigns

of ______________________ (Ph __________) hereinafter called the Buyer, hereby agree that the Seller shall sell and the Buyer shall buy the following described property UPON THE TERMS AND CONDITIONS HEREINAFTER SET FORTH, which shall include the STANDARDS FOR REAL ESTATE TRANSACTIONS set forth on reverse side of this contract

1. LEGAL DESCRIPTION of real estate located in Lee County County, Florida (Include Street address, if applicable) 931 Orange Grove Blvd. Sec. 4 Unit 1 s/d Tropic Isles

This sale is subject to the following special conditions Seller is aware purchaser is a registered Real Estate salesperson

Personal property included in accordance with attached inventory, or as follows range, refrigerator, wall a/c

Seller represents that the property can be used for the following purposes: Residential

2. PURCHASE PRICE AND METHOD OF PAYMENT

$ 100.00 deposit paid to and held by Home Hunters, Inc., upon acceptance pending closing

$ ---------

$ 15967.00 approximate principal balance on first mortgage, if any. Mortgage holder United Companies Mortgage
Interest 18 % per annum. Method of payment 316 PITI

$ 4533.00 Purchase money note and mortgage to Seller. Interest 10 % per annum
Method of payment 180 day note, principal and interest due: 180 days from date of closing

$ -0- Cash or Cashier's check on closing and delivery of deed (or such greater or lesser amount as may be necessary to complete payment or purchase price after credits, adjustments or prorations.)

$ 20,[illegible]00.00 Total purchase price

3. FINANCING. If the purchase price or any part thereof is to be financed by a third party loan, this Contract for Sale and Purchase, is conditioned upon the Buyer obtaining a firm commitment for said loan within ______ days from date hereof, at an interest rate not to exceed ______ %, term of ______ years; and in the principal amount of $ ______. Buyer agrees to make application for, and to use reasonable diligence to obtain said loan.

4. TIME FOR ACCEPTANCE. If this contract is not executed by the Seller and Buyer on or before February 12, 1983 the aforesaid deposit shall be, at the option of the Buyer, returned to him and this agreement shall be null and void. The date of contract, for purposes of performance, shall be regarded as the date when the last one of the Seller and Buyer has signed this contract.

5. CLOSING DATE: Except as provided in Paragraph 6 hereof, this contract shall be closed and deed delivered on 21 day of February, 19 83, or 30 days from date of this contract, whichever is later, and possession shall be delivered on or before Day of closing

6. PRORATIONS: Taxes, insurance, interest, rents and other expenses and revenue of said property shall be prorated as of the date of closing.

7. EVIDENCE OF TITLE. Within ______ days from date of this contract, the Seller shall, at his expense, deliver to the Buyer or his attorney: day of closing (Check either para. (1) or (2)):

_____ (1) A complete abstract of title prepared by a reputable abstract firm, purporting to be an accurate synopsis of the instruments affecting the title to that real property recorded in public records of that county to the date of this contract, showing in the Seller a marketable title in accordance with title standards adopted from time to time by the Florida Bar, subject only to liens and encumbrances specified in Paragraph 8 and those which shall be discharged by Seller at or before closing.

XXX (2) A title insurance commitment issued by a qualified title insuror acceptable to Buyer agreeing to issue to the Buyer, upon recording of the deed hereafter mentioned, an owner guarantee policy in the amount of the purchase price insuring the title of the Buyer to that real property without exceptions or qualifications other than those set forth in this contract.

The Buyer shall have fifteen (15) days from date of receipt of abstract or title insurance commitment to examine the same. If said title is found to be defective, the Buyer shall, within said fifteen (15) day period, notify the Seller in writing specifying the defects. If the said defects render the title unmarketable, the Seller shall have ninety (90) days from the receipt of such notice to cure the defects. If after reasonable diligence Seller shall not have cured the defects, Buyer shall have the option: (1) accepting the title as it then is, or (2) demanding a refund of all monies paid hereunder which shall forthwith be returned to the Buyer, and thereupon the Buyer and the Seller shall be released of all further obligations under this contract.

8. RESTRICTIONS AND EASEMENTS: Buyer shall take title subject to restrictions of record, zoning ordinances and public utility easements of record; provided that none of the foregoing materially interfere with the aforesaid agreed use of the property.

9. CONVEYANCE: Seller shall convey title to the aforesaid property to the Buyer by statutory warranty deed subject to matters contained in this contract and taxes for the year of closing. Conveyance to be made to Purchaser or as otherwise instructed.

10. TYPEWRITTEN OR HANDWRITTEN PROVISIONS: Typewritten or handwritten provisions inserted in this form shall control all printed provisions in conflict therewith.

11. OCCUPANCY: Seller represents that there are no parties in occupancy other than Seller, but if property is intended to be rented or occupied beyond closing, the fact and terms thereof shall be stated herein, and the tenant(s) shall be disclosed pursuant to Standard H. Seller agrees to deliver occupancy of property at time of closing unless otherwise specified above. If occupancy is to be delivered prior to closing, Buyer assumes all risk of loss to property from date of occupancy, shall be responsible and liable for maintenance thereof from said date, and shall be deemed to have accepted the property, real, and personal, in its existing condition as of time of taking occupancy unless otherwise noted in writing.

12. ASSIGNABILITY: (CHECK ONE) Buyer ☒ may assign ☐ may not assign, Contract.

13. OTHER AGREEMENTS: No agreements or representations, unless incorporated in this contract, shall be binding upon any of the parties.

WITNESSES: (Two are required.)

____

____

As to Buyer

Executed by Buyer on Feb 7, 1983

[illegible] (SEAL)

[illegible] (SEAL)

Buyer

WITNESSES: (Two are required.)

____

Elmer [illegible]

As to Seller

Executed by Seller on ______________________

______________________ (SEAL)

Joseph A. Molina (SEAL)

Seller

Deposit received on Feb 23, 1983 to be held subject to this contract. By: Home Hunters Inc. Jim [illegible]
(Broker, Attorney, Other)

COMMISSION TO BROKER: Seller acknowledges the employment of Home Hunters, Inc., as broker and agrees to pay said broker the sum of $ as listed As commission for finding the Buyer and in the event the sale is closed. In the event of a default by the Buyer, one-half of the money paid or to be paid the Seller pursuant to Standard V of this contract shall be paid to the broker, provided, however, the same shall not exceed the full amount of the commission. If the transaction shall not be closed because of refusal or failure of Seller to perform, the Seller shall pay said fee in full to Broker on demand.

______________________ (SEAL)

______________________ (SEAL)

This is a legally binding contract. If not fully understood, seek competent advice.

Watch for Buy Downs
They Want the Cash—They Want the Cash!

I apologize for moving backwards here, but I have to return to the two duplexes we bought in February. I had given you some reasons on why we didn't sell these for the quick $10,000 profit. I believed it was wiser to put a home improvement loan on them and pocket some tax free money, instead of taking the short term gain money. Well, at this writing, we still had not done that. We had them painted and readied to rent, but we weren't pressured to pull any money out.

The day came when I wasn't really busy tracking deals and we were in between some rehab projects. I decided to call some banks about a home improvement loan. To my surprise, it was easy. My banker and mortgage broker (I was comparing rates) said they had money available at 15% for ten years and one point.

Great, I thought. Now all I had to do was prepare some estimates totaling $15,000, along with my financial statement, and apply. Everything was fine until I told him we had a second mortgage. "I'm sorry, Russ," he said. "We can't do it in a third position. You would have to get the second mortgage holder to subordinate to a third position, so we could have the second."

Easier said than done. We got the owner to sell for $24,000 below market value, with no money down, plus a good interest rate. He'll hit the roof and think we're wheeling him if I ask him to go to a third position. I did not want to jeopardize our rapport with him. He had more income properties to sell and already indicated he would give us first shot at them. The funny thing is, he knows our terms.

What did we do? Before I tell you about Dan's brainstorm, let me clear up some things here about home improvement loans.

The best ones to locate are the FHA Title I loans. These are insured by the federal government, so it is a safe loan for the bank. With a Title I loan, you can have a second mortgage and still qualify. Here in Southwest Florida, I have yet to find a bank that offers Title I loans. They all quit doing Title I's for various reasons. This is one of the few areas in the country that doesn't use them. The banks write their own loans. It makes things a little tougher, but it's just one of those small hurdles you either jump over, go under, or get around to keep moving forward.

Getting back to Dan's brainstorm. I called and told him the bank would not take a third position on a home improvement loan. His attitude matched mine. He didn't really want to upset the applecart with the owner either. "Let's sleep on it," he said, "and discuss it tomorrow."

The phone rang rather early the next morning. It was 7:00 a.m., and Dan was talking a mile a minute about this great idea. He couldn't sleep the night before and had been up since 4:00 a.m. working numbers on the owner of the CBS duplexes deal (or no deal, I should say).

I'm usually up at 5:00 a.m. every morning, so I was already in my office (the one built behind my house) when he called. I was wide awake and getting very excited about his idea. The more he talked, the better it sounded.

Dan had run an amortization on the money we owed him. If you remember, we bought the properties (both duplexes) for $76,000. We put no money down (except closing costs), and we assumed $32,000 from the bank at 8%. Carter held $44,000 in a second mortgage at 11% for 20 years.

Dan's numbers indicated that we should call the owner and ask him to take $30,000 cash money for his $44,000 mortgage. If he put the money in a 10% interest bearing investment (money market funds or a super now account), he would earn an amount equal to what we owed him seven years sooner! By discounting his mortgage $12,000 for us, he would get $30,000 cash immediately. If he puts it in a bank that earns10% interest, he would get the total amount of our monthly payments on the 20 year mortgage in only 13 years. If he gets a better interest-bearing investment, he would get an equal amount even sooner. He also gets $30,000 immediately and has zero interest in the property, 100% cashed out.

It was a good deal for him and a good deal for us. If the owner agreed, we would end up buying these properties for $14,000 less; a total price of $31,000 per duplex. These duplexes would sell for $50,000 easily. That is a $38,000 profit!

Now, where did we get $30,000 to pay the owner off? That was easy. The bank had a fixed 8% mortgage on each duplex of $16,000. They would love to get rid of those low interest rates and turn it into 12% or 13%, wouldn't they? Of course!

Dan and I applied for a new mortgage of $40,000 on each duplex,

Dan and I applied for a new mortgage of $40,000 on each duplex, which is 80% of the appraised value. Most banks will lend 80%. Now, we had a new mortgage of $80,000 at 13 % for 25 years. Our payment was $902 per month. If you look back, you'll see the old payment on both the first and second mortgage totaled $771. So, we've raised the payment by $131. We still had about $238 per month positive cash flow, though.

What about the loan proceeds? We received $80,000 from the bank. We immediately gave the bank the $32,000 we owed, leaving $48,000. We then paid Carter $30,000 which cashed him out completely, and left us with. . . ? C'mon, you mean we put $18,000 in tax free money in our pockets? Now I'm really excited!

I'll bet when a set plan backfires, more money is made and more creativeness surfaces than would ever happen under normal circumstances. We were under the gun because of the bank's policy on home improvement loans. It bugged Dan, so he got up in the middle of the night and came up with a better, cleaner, simpler way to make more money on the deal.

Be on the lookout for circumstances to buy down a mortgage. They need the cash, they need the cash! Caution—don't use the word "discount" when you ask. It's a negative sounding word and it intimidates a mortgage holder. You must show him the benefits he'll receive by taking this much cash "today." If you both can win, you'll have a deal. A helpful hint: make sure you get him to sign a 90 day commitment to take the discount.

How to Use a Prospectus to Get Loans

While reading the local real estate magazine one day, Dan located an old Spanish-style house for sale. It was advertised at $110,000 with $20,000 down. It didn't look like a very good buy as listed, but it was around the corner from a seven unit building that I owned. Dan met with the owner/broker, who turned out to be a pretty flexible seller. The owner had tried to make the home into a rooming house at one time, and had not had good luck with it at all. At their meeting, the owner indicated several ways that the property could be financed.

Dan told me of the meeting, but we put this deal on the back burner. I was primarily interested in accumulating more multi-family units. This Spanish house didn't seem to fit the bill. At that time we had a pretty full schedule of properties to see and others to close on. One day we were down in the area and had a little free time, so we decided to stop and take a look and investigate its possibilities.

As we went through the building, I was impressed. It must have been a beautiful, stately home at one time. The hardwood floors were in excellent shape, as were the walls and ceilings. There were three baths and at least ten rooms. Initially, we thought we could partition it off and make five small apartments. The renovation costs would be very high. We would have to get a good price and terms on this one to make it profitable. We kicked several offers around for a few days. During that time, we came up with a much better idea for the Spanish house on Woodford Avenue.

One of the best money making strategies in real estate is the "highest and best use" concept. Simply stated, the "highest and best use" means taking a piece of property and maximizing its potential in today's marketplace.

Woodford would, one day, make a beautiful office building with the expansion of our downtown area. At the time, however, it was not quite ready for that change. Also, changing it into apartments would be very costly.

Keeping in mind the future plans for offices, we finally settled on the present highest and best use. Woodford would make a perfect ten unit rooming house. There were three baths and one central kitchen. Basically, all we would have to do is partition some of the rooms and buy ten beds, lamps, dressers and night stands. This idea maximized and justified the purchase in two ways. First, ten rooms would bring in, at $45 per week, $23,400 per year. This would cover all of our debt, plus a $15,000 home improvement loan (of which only $7,500 would go to renovation) and give us an $800 per month net positive cash flow. At the same time, we would partition the building for easy conversion to offices when the time was right. We could even have our own offices there.

The following are the actual contracts with the seller and the prospectus for the $15,000 home improvement loan from the bank. As you will see, we purchased the property for $90,000 with no money down. We made payments of $285 per month for the first six months. Then, we paid interest only payments on the third mortgage held by the seller ($300 per month) plus the $285 for the next six months. The seller is in a third position so we could get the home improvement

PROSPECTUS
1630 WOODFORD AVENUE
FT. MYERS, FLORIDA 3/4/83

The following is a detailed format for the renovation of the above mentioned property in Lee County.

This property is the homestead of James Evans lending historic value on the National Register.

This property was also used by the Lee County Mental Health Clinic, which would lend credence to the structural soundness and the plumbing and electric status.

It is our intent to rehabilitate this property, keeping it's original charm intact. Dividing the interior into a rooming accomodation for senior citizens, while maintaining the historic value of the property, seems to be the highest and best use for the aforementioned.

The building to the rear of the property, which was once a garage, has been renovated to some extent for office space. There is over 300 sq. feet which we intend to complete for our personal downtown office.

As per the survey you will notice an abundance of parking availability. A definite plus for downtown office faciltles.

Our plans for the division of the interior will be done so we may , in the future with little cost, redivide the building for first class office space. If the highest and best use at that time demands the change our plans presently will accomodate same.

Any questions pertaining to this project may be directed to Daniel M. Kelly or Russell A. Whitney.

Russell A. Whitney
Daniel M. Kelly

1630 WOODFORD AVENUE, FT. MYERS
Prepared by: Russ Whitney - Dan Kelly

PROJECTED RENT ROLL STATEMENT & DEBIT

The figures stated below are believed to be conservatively accurate. Projections are based upon current market rents within a half mile of Woodford Ave in similar accomodations. Over 40 apartment units currently being managed by R. Whitney & D. Kelly in the immediate area were surveyed and averaged.

RENTS #
1. $45.00 6. $45.00
2. $45.00 7. 45.00
3. 45.00 8. 45.00
4. 45.00 9. 45.00
5. 45.00 10. 45.00

Gross monthly rents -------$1,935.00
Gross yearly rents --------23,220.00
Rents are based on 4.3 weeks per month and 12 months per year. Rents are conservative compared to $50.00 & $70.00 in comparables.

DEBT SERVICE
1. Taxes ------ $600.00 Note: this year under present homestead - $200.00
2. Insurance -- 500.00 (maximum)
3. Water, Sew - 1,000.00
4. License & Permits ----- 46.00
5. Vacancy --(3%) 696.60 Note: Our present vacancy ratio in over 40 units is less than 1%.

YEARLY - $2,842.00
MONTHLY-/ 236.83

MORTGAGE INFO
First Mortgage - $32,983.00 @ $285.33 per month
Graduation Scale - a. October 1, 1983 - payment escalates to $585.83
b. April 1, 1984 - " " " $889.11
and remains at that amount for the duration of the loan and mortgage.

PROJECTED NET CASH FLOW - Year one - $16,954.04 less mtg. increase - $15,154
Monthly --- 1,412.83 " " " 1,262
Year two ---- 9,708.68 at peak escalation
Monthly ----- 809.05 " " "

*** Note no rent increase has been factored

The above projections show a rent roll which will easily support a $15,000.00 Renovation Loan @ 14% for a 10 year period. That is the subject of the following.

Russell B Whitney
Donal M Kelly

BEFORE

AFTER

This property was the first in which the rooming house concept was used. It was converted to ten rooms and created tremendous cash flow, which every beginning investor needs to get started.

RE/MAX
REALTORS®
of Fort Myers, Inc.
5448 South U.S. 41
Fort Myers, Fl. 33907
RE/MAX
Above the Crowd!
(813) 936-4494
prc Computer Network
"An International network of individually owned and operated real estate offices."
FOUR BEDROOM, two bath in Camelot. Large garage with workshop area. Cathedral ceilings in living room. Assumable $77,000 9¼% mortgage. Owner will consider 2nd mortgage. $127,000.
OLD FLORIDA MANSION. Built into 7 rental units. Grossing $18,000/year. Needs some cosmetic repairs. $110,000. $20,000 down, 30 year mortgage, 9% for first 3 years.
SPANISH TYPE HOME on Woodford. 4,000 sq. ft., 10 ft ceilings, natural wood floors. Ideal office building. Extra lot for 5 residential or office spaces. Needs remodeling. $110,000. $20,000 down, 30 year mortgage, 9% for first 3 years.
CORNER LOT
Pine Manor. Variance needed— easily attainable. $7,000. $2,000 down, balance over 3 years at 10%.
265+ FEET ON CALOOSAHATCHEE
Producing $55,000 per year. 10 mobile homes, 2 duplexes, 1 triplex. Excellent area for condominium in future. Located next to a major marina. MOVE FAST TO GET THIS ONE!
3½ ACRES ZONED INDUSTRIAL
In central area of Naples. All or part. Terms available. Includes releases and subordination to a bona fide lending institution. $3.50 per sq. ft.
THREE MOBILE HOMES IN PEACEFUL PINES
Priced from $20,000 to $24,000. $2,000 down each, 15 years at 12%. 75x125 lot.
BRAND NEW HOME
3 bedrooms, 1 bath. 1100 sq. ft., south. $48,900, $3,000 down, 10% financing for 25 years.
FOR MORE INFORMATION ON ANY OF THESE FINE PROPERTIES, CONTACT: RICHARD W. BIRBECK, President, at (813) 936-4494 or, after hours, (813) 332-7711.

Proposal and Contract

GENERAL CONTRACTOR

SOUTHWEST MANAGEMENT AND DEVELOPMENT
CAPE CORAL, FORT MYERS, LEE COUNTY
2520 S.E. 8th Place, Cape Coral, Fla.
574-4815 549-0451 574-8121

GENERAL CONTRACTOR

1

PROPOSAL SUBMITTED TO	PHONE	DATE
Mr. Whitney / Kelly	549-0451	3/4/83
STREET	JOB NAME	
1630 Woodford St.	Same	
CITY STATE AND ZIP CODE	JOB LOCATION	
Ft. Myers, Fla.	Same	

ARCHITECT	DATE OF PLANS		JOB PHONE
RW	3/3/83	XXXXXXXXXXXXXXXX XX	X X XXXX

We hereby submit specifications and estimates for

#1. Build a 9'x9'10" stud and sheetrock partition. Tape and paint. Provide for and install 1 32" pre-hung door. Install doorknob and single bolt lock set
#2. Build a 9' x 9'10" stud and sheetrock partition. Tape and paint. Provide for and install 1 32" pre-hung door. Install doorknob and single bolt lock set.
#3. Build a 10' x 13'10" studm and sheetrock partition. Tape and paint. Provic for and install 1 32" pre-hung door. Install new doorknob and single bolt lock set. Install a 9' x 13'10" commercial remnant carpet. (Choice of color. $4.99 yc
#4. Build a 10' x 13'10" stud and sheetrock partition. Tape and paint. Install a 32" pre-hung door. Install doorknob and single bolt lock set. Provide and install a commercial remnant carpet, 12' x 14'. (color choice @ $4.99 yd.) Block present window opening with built in bookshelves. (12" pine & stain) Packer
#5.. Provide and install a 13' x 17' commercial remnant carpet, (color choice $4.99 yd). One 5' patch, sheetrock and stucco ceiling and seal. Remove three ceiling fans, cap wiring and cover. Repaint room, three gallons, apprx. 6 hours labor on paint. Block off door to unit #6 with a 4' x 8' sheetrock partition. Rip and replace moldings. Tape and paint.
#6 Paint ceiling. Provide and install a 10' x 14' commercial remnant carpet. (color choice @$4.99 yd.). Block off door to unit #5 with a 4' x 8' sheetrock partition. Rip and replace moldings. Tape and paint.
#7. 2/3' sheetrock patches and stucco over entire ceiling. Provide and install a 12½ x 14' commercilm remnant carpet. (choice of color @ $4.99 yd.). Install wood panelling on north wall. (choice of panel $10.00 per sheet). Install 9 1' mirrored tiles on south wall to cover old partition marks. Paint remaining walls. Install new doorknob and single bolt lock set. Block off door to unit #8 with a 4' x 8' sheetrock partition. Rip and replace molding. Tape and paint. Replace a 29" x 39" pice of glass on east window. Secure light switch from

We Propose hereby to furnish material and labor — complete in accordance with above specifications, for the sum of:

dollars ($)

Payment to be made as follows:

All material is guaranteed to be as specified. All work to be completed in a workmanlike manner according to standard practices. Any alteration or deviation from above specifications involving extra costs will be executed only upon written orders, and will become an extra charge over and above the estimate. All agreements contingent upon strikes, accidents or delays beyond our control. Owner to carry fire, tornado and other necessary insurance.

Authorized Signature

Note: This proposal may be withdrawn by us if not accepted within ______ days.

Acceptance of Proposal — The above prices, specifications and conditions are satisfactory and are hereby accepted. You are authorized to do the work as specified. Payment will be made as outlined above.

Signature Continued

Signature

Date of Acceptance

Proposal and Contract

(2)

PROPOSAL SUBMITTED TO		PHONE	DATE
STREET		JOB NAME	
CITY, STATE AND ZIP CODE		JOB LOCATION	
ARCHITECT	DATE OF PLANS		JOB PHONE

We hereby submit specifications and estimates for CONTINUED - CONTINUED - CONTINUED - CONTINUED -
ceiling to stationary wall position. Build a stud and sheetrock closet acc-
omidation, apprx 5' x 8'.
#9. Sheetrock patch on ceiling and stucco in entirety. Install a '2½ x '4'
commercial remnant carpet. (choice of color - $4.99 yd.). Install 9/'' mirror
tiles on south wall to cover partition matks. Block of bathroom entry with a
4' x 8' shetrock partition. Rip moldings. Block off entry to unit #7 from
closet, with a 4 x 8' sheetrock partition. Rip moldings. Install new doorknob
and single bolt lock set.
#9 Block bathroom entrance with a 4' x 8' sheetrock partition. Rip moldings.
Tape and paint. Stucco ceiling. Repaint in entirety. Install new doorknob
and single bolt lock set. Install a '2'3" x '7' commercial remnant carpet.
(choice of color - $4.99 yd.).
#10. block entry to unit #9 with a 4' x 8' panel and stud partition. Rip
moldings: Build a stud and sheetrock closet, 5' x 8'. Install new single bolt
lock set. (doorknob looks salvagable, can possibly rekey).
BATHROOMS UPSTAIRS - Install new doorknob set. Replace tile floor with '' vinyl
7½' x ''. Provide and install ' Scotty's medicine cabinet, ($'9.95). Repaint
upper half of bathroom. Replace apprx 5 ceramic tiles. Block off inside door
to unit #8 & #9 with a 4' x 8' sheetrock partiition. Rip moldings and repaint.
Provide and install ' light swithc cover. Provide and install a new ceramic
toilet tissue holder.
#2 BATHROOM - Replace ceramic tiles inside bath enclosure. Apprx. '' X 5½'/
Stucco upper half of all walls, ceiling. Replace washers in leaky sink faucets
Install new doorknob set, (locking).
UPPER HALLWAY - Patch cracks, repaint in entirety. Sand floors and cover with
polyurethane finish. Install runner carpet 3' width apprx 80', includes stair

We Propose hereby to furnish material and labor — complete in accordance with above specifications, for the sum of:

_____ dollars ($ _____)

Payment to be made as follows

All material is guaranteed to be as specified. All work to be completed in a workmanlike manner according to standard practices. Any alteration or deviation from above specifications involving extra costs will be executed only upon written orders, and will become an extra charge over and above the estimate. All agreements contingent upon strikes, accidents or delays beyond our control. Owner to carry fire, tornado and other necessary insurance.

Authorized Signature _____

Note: This proposal may be withdrawn by us if not accepted within _____ days.

Acceptance of Proposal — The above prices, specifications and conditions are satisfactory and are hereby accepted. You are authorized to do the work as specified. Payment will be made as outlined above.

Signature Continued

Signature _____

Date of Acceptance _____

Proposal and Contract

(3)

PROPOSAL SUBMITTED TO	PHONE	DATE

STREET	JOB NAME

CITY, STATE AND ZIP CODE	JOB LOCATION

ARCHITECT	DATE OF PLANS		JOB PHONE

We hereby submit specifications and estimates for CONTINUED - CONTINUED - CONTINUED - CONTINUED

Repaint tannister and varnish top rail. Replace [illegible] light switch cover, Replace one closet door.
Lower Hallway - Cover with polyurethane finish. Paint kitchen and halls. Provide and install 7' of countertop on unfinished cabinets. Replace missing kitchen cabinet door,
BATHROOM DOWNSTAIRS - Secure shower stall. Finish partition to rear porch to ceiling.
OUTSIDE BUILDING - Pressure clean and paint. Repair front porch with tar and gravel.
REAR BUILDING - 30[illegible] square ft. of carpet installed. Finish bathroom with new vinyl [illegible]' tiles and door. Replace hot water heater. Install kitchen sink and faucet and drain set. Replace rear door with a prehung and new doorknob and single bolt lock set. Pressure clean exterior and repaint in entirety. Remove assorted debris from grounds surrounding both buildings.

XX All agreements between contractor and owner have been specified in this estimate. Their are no other written or oral representations by either party other than those contained herein.
XXXXXXXXXXXXXXXXXXXXXXXXXXXXXXXXXXXXXXXXXXXXXXXXXXXXXXXXXXXXXXXXX
XXXXXXXXXXXXXXXXXXXXXXXXXXXXXXXXXXXXXXXXXXXXXXXXXXXXXXXXXXXXXXXXX
XXXXXXXXXXXXXXXXXXXXXXXXXXXXXXXXXXXXXXXXXXXXXXXXXXXXXXXXXXXXXXXXX
XXXXXXXXXXXXXXXXXXXXXXXXXXXXXXXXXXXXXXXXXXXXXXXXXXXXXXXXXXXXXXXXX

We Propose hereby to furnish material and labor — complete in accordance with above specifications, for the sum of:
seventeen thousand, seven hundred and seventy five dollars ($ 17,775.00)

Payment to be made as follows:
IN FULL AS PER AGREEMENT, TAX INCLUDED, LABOR INCLUDED, MATRIAL INCLUDED

All material is guaranteed to be as specified. All work to be completed in a workmanlike manner according to standard practices. Any alteration or deviation from above specifications involving extra costs will be executed only upon written orders, and will become an extra charge over and above the estimate. All agreements contingent upon strikes, accidents or delays beyond our control. Owner to carry fire, tornado and other necessary insurance.

Authorized Signature ______ GENERAL CONTRACTOR

Note: This proposal may be withdrawn by us if not accepted within 30 days.

Acceptance of Proposal — The above prices, specifications and conditions are satisfactory and are hereby accepted. You are authorized to do the work as specified. Payment will be made as outlined above.

Signature ______

Signature ______

Date of Acceptance ______

Proposal and Contract

SOUTH.EST MANAGEMENT AND DEVELOPMENT
CAPE CORAL, FT. MYERS, LEE COUNTY
2520 S.E. 8th Place, Cape Coral, Fla
574-48·5 549-045· 574-8·2·

PROPOSAL SUBMITTED TO		PHONE	DATE
Mr. hitney/Kelly		549-045·	3/5/83
STREET		JOB NAME	
1630 .oodford St.		Same	
CITY STATE AND ZIP CODE		JOB LOCATION	
Ft. Myers, Fla		Same	
ARCHITECT	DATE OF PLANS		JOB PHONE
	3/4/83	XXXXX XXXX XXX XXXXXXX	XXXX X X X

We hereby submit specifications and estimates for

The following is a listing of furnishings which is included ~~in~~ in the estimated, contracted price of $17,775.00. The owners will be soley responsible for the purchase, delivery and quality of same.

AS FOLLOWS:

1. 10 full size beds
2. 10 dressers
3. 10 nightstands
4. 10 easy chairs
5. 10 lamps

CURTAINS -
1. 3½ x 4½' (2 sets) apt. #1 & #2
2. 5' x 10' (1 set) apt #3
5. 2 - 3 x 4' sets
6. 7' x ··' set
7. 2 - 4' x 7' sets
8. 3 - 4' x 6' drape sets
9. 2 - 4 x 6' sets & 1 - 5 x 6' set
10. Miscellaneous - 3 - 4 x 6' sets,

3 - office desks and chairs for rear building. 3 - phones. 2 sets of 4 drawer file cabinets.

We Propose hereby to furnish material and labor — complete in accordance with above specifications, for the sum of:

dollars ($)

Payment to be made as follows

All material is guaranteed to be as specified. All work to be completed in a workmanlike manner according to standard practices. Any alteration or deviation from above specifications involving extra costs will be executed only upon written orders, and will become an extra charge over and above the estimate. All agreements contingent upon strikes, accidents or delays beyond our control. Owner to carry fire, tornado and other necessary insurance.

Authorized Signature

Note: This proposal may be withdrawn by us if not accepted within days.

Acceptance of Proposal — The above prices, specifications and conditions are satisfactory and are hereby accepted. You are authorized to do the work as specified. Payment will be made as outlined above.

Date of Acceptance

Signature

Signature

EXHIBIT 'A'

A lot or parcel of land lying in Lot 4, Block 9, Homestead of James Evans Section 13, Township 44 South, Range 24 East, City of Ft. Myers as shown on a plat recorded in Plat Book 1, at page 23, Lee County records, and in Lots 9 and 11, Hugh MacDonald, Jr.'s Subdivision as shown on a plat recorded in Plat Book 1, at page 39 of said public records, which lot or parcel is described as follows:

Beginning at the axle marking the northerlymost corner of said Lot 9; thence run southeasterly along the northeasterly line of said Lot 9 and the southwesterly line of Woodford Avenue (46.25 feet wide) for 99.84 feet to the southeasterly line of a concrete sidewalk 3 feet wide; thence continue along the southwesterly line of said Woodford Avenue and the northeasterly line of Lot 11, Hugh MacDonald, Jr.'s Subdivision for 8.46 feet to a steel pin now set; thence deflect 96°18'40" to the right and run southwesterly for 80.12 feet to a steel pin now set at the easterly junction of the southwesterly prolongation of the aforementioned 3 feet wide sidewalk and a second sidewalk also 3 feet wide running northwest; thence deflect 22°42'12" to the right and run westerly for 13.58 feet to a steel pin now set at the westerly junction of two other sidewalks, one being 3.9 feet wide and running southeast; the second being 3 feet wide and running northeast; thence deflect 28°20'33" to the left and run southwesterly along the northwesterly edge and the prolongation thereof of the latter sidewalk, 3 feet wide, for 57.17 feet to an intersection with the southwesterly line of lands described in deed recorded in Deed Book 194 at page 124 of said public records; thence run northwesterly along said southwesterly line for 50.0 feet more or less to a concrete monument marking the westerlymost corner of said lands; thence run northeasterly along the northwesterly line of said lands for 10.8 feet to a concrete monument on the southwesterly line of said Lot 9, Hugh MacDonald, Jr.'s Subdivision; thence run northwesterly along said southwesterly line for 41.5 feet to a concrete monument marking the westerlymost corner of said Lot 9; thence run northeasterly along the northwesterly line of said Lot 9 for 138 feet to the Point of Beginning.

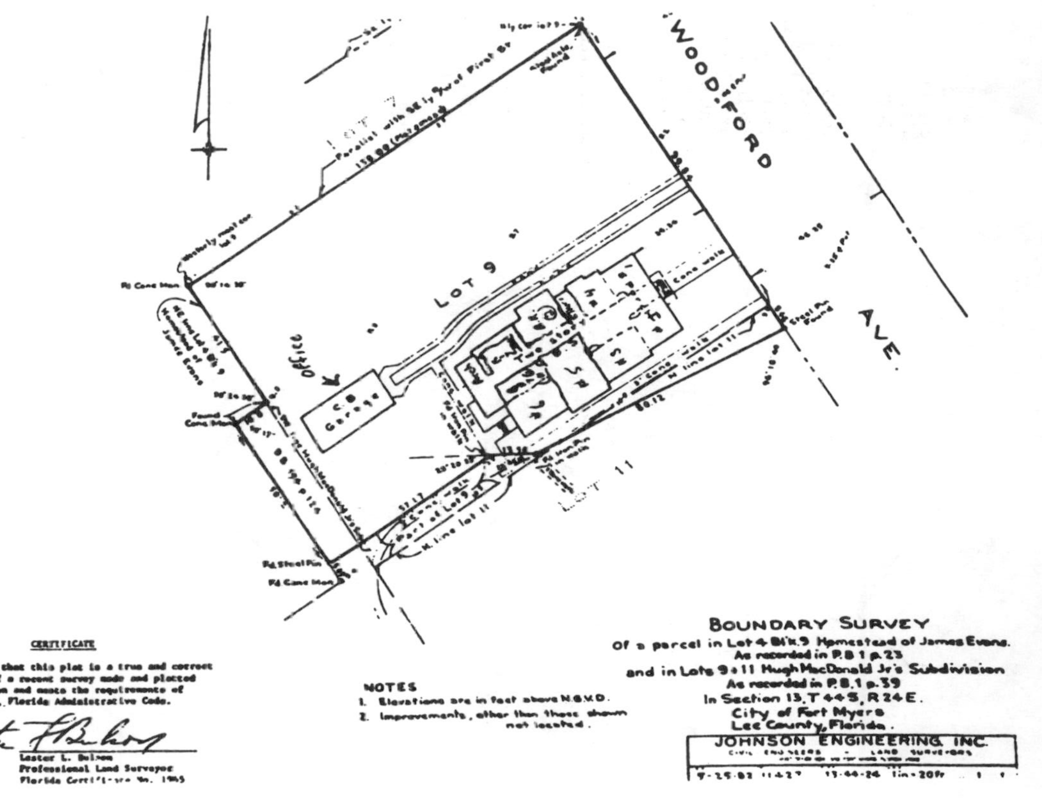
WOODFORD AVE.
LOT 7
LOT 9
LOT 11
Office
C.B. Garage
CERTIFICATE
I hereby certify that this plat is a true and correct representation of a recent survey made and platted under my direction and meets the requirements of Chapter: 21 HH-6, Florida Administrative Code.
Professional Land Surveyor
NOTES
1. Elevations are in feet above N.G.V.D.
2. Improvements, other than those shown not located.
BOUNDARY SURVEY
Of a parcel in Lot 4 Blk.9 Homestead of James Evans.
As recorded in P.B 1 p.23
and in Lots 9 & 11 Hugh MacDonald Jr's Subdivision
As recorded in P.B.1 p.39
In Section 13, T 44 S, R 24 E.
City of Fort Myers
Lee County, Florida.
JOHNSON ENGINEERING, INC.

1st FLOOR

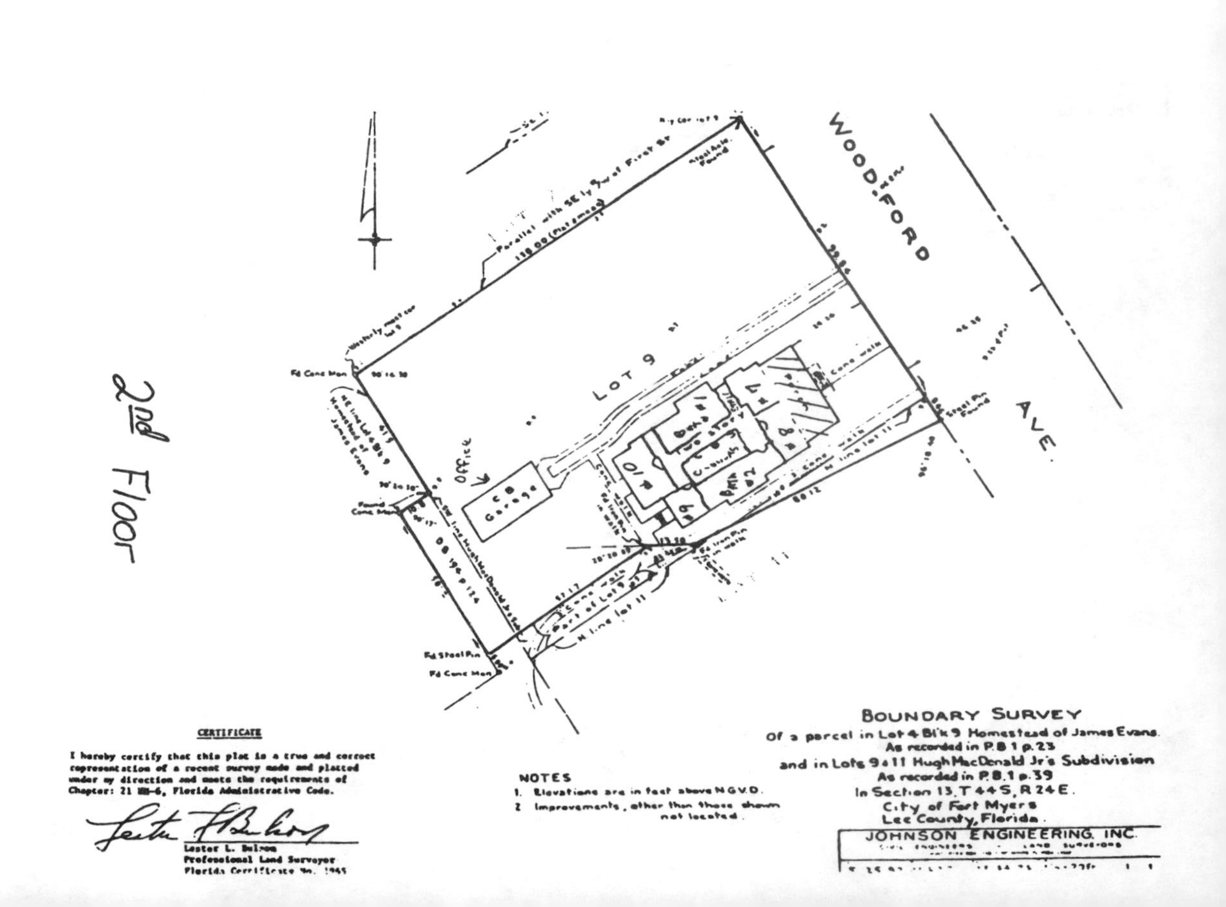
WOODFORD AVE.
LOT 9
Office
Garage
2nd Floor
CERTIFICATE
I hereby certify that this plat is a true and correct representation of a recent survey made and platted under my direction and meets the requirements of Chapter: 21 HH-6, Florida Administrative Code.
Professional Land Surveyor
NOTES
1. Elevations are in feet above N.G.V.D.
2. Improvements, other than those shown not located.
BOUNDARY SURVEY
Of a parcel in Lot 4 Blk 9 Homestead of James Evans.
As recorded in P.B 1 p.23
and in Lots 9 & 11 Hugh MacDonald Jr's Subdivision
As recorded in P.B.1 p.39
In Section 13, T 44 S, R 24 E.
City of Fort Myers
Lee County, Florida.
JOHNSON ENGINEERING, INC.

loan. The bank required a second position. After the first year we turned the whole mortgage amount, with the seller, into a 30 year fixed mortgage. Talk about creative! This may seem a bit complicated at first, but if you sit back and absorb it, it makes sense. Much of this creativeness was the seller's idea. He wanted out of the property and wanted to be sure we made good money so he wouldn't get it back.

The prospectus took all of a half a day to prepare. Banks love this type of preparation. It's really simple to put together. I took the prospectus to three banks and one mortgage broker. The savings and loans were impressed and we had two offers from interested lenders.

Notice how I drew up the prospectus. Why do you think the lenders were so willing to make us a loan? If you'll note on the projected rent roll statement, there is no mention of a third mortgage. I do show our payment escalation, which includes the payment on the third, but not the amount. It looks as if we only owe $32,000 on $110,000 property. Is that dishonest? No! It is not the bank's business if we have a third mortgage. As long as their money is protected in the second mortgage position, the bank's loan is safe. We don't need to billboard the fact that there will be a third mortgage. The seller had agreed not to record the third until we got the second mortgage from the bank.

Some of you may not agree with that tactic, so consider these circumstances. Suppose we only have the first mortgage. Then, we got the bank to loan us some money and put a second mortgage on the building. So far, so good. Everything is fine. Now, we find a private party or a mortgage broker to lend us some money, but he wants to lien our property with a third mortgage. Is that all right? Of course. The bank could not care less if you put a third mortgage on the property. It is your responsibility to call the bank six months later and say, "Mr. Banker, I borrowed some money on it; they want to put a third mortgage on the property. Is that okay with you?" Well, of course that's ridiculous and again, I'm being somewhat facetious, but I just want you to understand, business is business. If I approached the banker and told him I bought the Spanish house for $90,000 with no money down and I needed to borrow $15,000 to boot, what do you think my chances would be for obtaining a loan? Exactly zero.

This is a chess game, a battle of brains and wits. The banker is always looking and probing, so be on guard, as you would if you were playing chess. Anticipate all of his questions ahead of time, and prepare your response. I always go over the meeting beforehand, word for word. I rehearse a presentation, and ask myself all of the questions I think the banker will ask. Then I answer as if we were already in the meeting. Sometimes he never asks all of the questions I think he will. It's fine if I'm over-prepared, but I never want to be caught under-prepared. By going over the meeting ahead of time, I have a distinct advantage when the game begins. I've already been at this meeting once, and the banker hasn't. In a battle of wits, my friend, he is unprepared!

Look back to that prospectus and make believe you're a banker. What questions would you ask? The prospectus answered about every possible question in advance. This is how I take the lender off guard. The only question I thought might pop up would be about the equity. I anticipated the banker might come right out and ask if I put $60,000 down on the property. I don't want to lie to him, so how did I answer? In fact, my hunch was correct. One lender did ask. I, of course, had the answer. I told him we traded some "things" which resulted in the equity reduction on this property. I also added that, "the bottom line is correct. We do have a $60,000 equity in this property presently, based on the purchase price of $90,000. However, Mr. Lender, the property will appraise for about $120,000, so that would actually give us a $90,000 equity." Do you know what he said? He said, "Mr. Whitney, we can lend you $15,000 at 14% for ten years. Will that be sufficient?"

What about morality and ethics in this case? Well, I told him the truth. We did do some trading. The seller traded us the property for no money down and we both traded agreements on not recording the third mortgage immediately. With those specific trades, we do, theoretically, have a big equity. The bottom line, cutting through all of the smoke is, the bank made a safe loan. We just did what had to be done to expedite it and make them feel good about lending the money. Ten people will have a beautiful rooming house to live in. Several carpenters and painters will have work, and we will have the Spanish house and a nice monthly cash flow. CHECKMATE!

The key is being prepared when you go looking for a loan. Bring your portfolio of properties that you presently own or manage, if you have any. Show the lender your experience in this area of investment. Always have a projected rent roll statement and estimates for work to be done. Do you know what one lender said upon our presentation of this deal? He said, "Well, it's a safe loan for us because of your equity. Your estimates total $17,775 and you only want to borrow $15,000. You're not shooting for the moon and you're going to put some of your own money in, too. That's good enough for us." Do you believe that? Our estimates were $17,775. If I had a contractor do all that work that figure would probably be close. By hiring unemployed carpenters and other tradesmen at $4.00 and $5.00 per hour and telling them what to do myself, I probably will get the job done for $6,500 to $7,500, and can pocket the rest. There is nothing wrong with getting several estimates, high and low. Borrow on the high estimates and hire the low estimates to do the work. You keep the difference as a consulting fee, or whatever you want to call it. Just make sure you get paid the smart way . . . the tax free way.

As you can see, we were building some strong momentum those first three weeks after the seminar. If you've been counting, we were also starting the gears turning to pull some big money out of these deals.

The following page is a signed copy of our offer on the Spanish house. This the bank did not see.

ADDENDUM A

Contract between Richard W. Birbeck and Russ Whitney and Dan Kelly.

1630 Woodford, Ft. Myers, Florida 33901

1. Buyer is to pay all closing costs. Including but not necessarily limited to Title Insurance, Recording of the Deed and Mortgage, and whatever other documents necessary to close this transaction.

2. The Buyer agrees to assume the First Mortgage of $32,983.00 and start making payments as of May 1, 1983. Payments are $285.33 per month. THE FIRST MORTGAGE IS A BALLOON MORTGAGE THAT BALLONS OCTOBER 1990. THE PRINCIPAL AMOUNT OF THE MORTGAGE WILL BE $28,056.00. THE SELLER AGREES TO SUBORDINATE THE PURCHASE MONEY THIRD MORTGAGE TO A NEW FIRST MORTGAGE IN THE AMOUNT NEEDED TO PAY OFF THE FIRST MORTGAGE AT THE TIME OF THE BALLOON PAYMENT. SAID LOAN TO BE TO A BONAFIDE LENDING INSTITUTION. THE SELLER AGREES TO DO THE ABOVE IF THE BUYER IS CURRENT ON THE PURCHASE MONEY THIRD MORTGAGE AND THE SECOND MORTGAGE AND HAS KEPT THE PROPERTY IN GOOD REPAIR.

3. Should the Buyer obtain a mortgage on subject property to do improvements, the Buyer will guarantee the amount of the loan personally. The method that will be used is to guarantee the top 25% of the purchase money third mortgage personally.

4. The Buyer agrees to do the necessary improvements and repairs to the property to bring it to a rentable condition. The Buyer agrees to submit such plans for renovation and the ultimate use of the property to the Seller for his approval.

5. The Buyer agrees to provide financial statements for Dan Kelly and Russ Whitney with this contract.

6. Buyer is aware that the Seller is a registered Real Estate Broker doing business in the state of Florida.

7. This contract will survive the documents at closing.

8. The Purchase Money Mortgage will be paid as follows; There will be a six month moratorium on interest and principal payments. Beginning October 1, 1983 the Buyers will pay $300.00 a month for six months. Since this will not be enough to cover the interest on the Purchase Money Third Mortgage $1600.00 will be added to the $57,000.00 bringing it to $58,600.00. Beginning April 1, 1984 this $58,600.00 Purchase Money Third Mortgage will be amortized over 30 years at 12% with the Principal and Interest payments of $603.78 per month for each month for 360 months.

9. The Buyer agrees to keep enough casualty insurance on the property naming the Seller as co-insured to cover the mortgages on subject property.

10. The Buyer and Seller warrant that there are no real estate commissions due on this transaction.

11. THE BUYER AGREES TO ACCEPT THE PROPERTY IN AS-IS CONDITION. THE BUYER IS AWARE THAT THE PROPERTY IS IN NEED OF RENOVATION AND REPAIR. THE SELLER DOES NOT WARRANT THE PROPERTY IN ANY WAY.

12. The Buyer is aware that the subject property contains approximately 1500 feet on the first floor, 1500 feet on the second floor and there is an attic on the third floor. There is also a small building that was once a garage that contains approximately 300 sq. ft. The Buyer is aware that the property can be used for multi-family or commercial use subject to the zoning and restrictions of the City of Fort Myers.

13. On or before the day of the closing the Second Mortgage to Sharon Hager shall be removed from the property.

14. Should the Buyers be making progress in obtaing the Home Improvement Loan, however have failed to do so by April 1 the closing date, the Seller will grant a 30 day extension. This will not preclude the Seller from taking a backup contract on subject property.

15. The Sellers Purchase Money Third Mortgage will be an Assumable Mortgage however the Seller retains the right to approve the new mortgagee and approval will not be unreasonably withheld. The Seller is making this transaction with Dan Kelly and Russ Whitney because of their expertise in renovating older properties. The financial strength and the expertise of a potential new buyer should be of a similar nature as the purchasers of this contract.

WITNESSES:

______________________ ______________________ (Buyer)

______________________ ______________________ (Buyer)

WITNESSES:

______________________ ______________________ (Seller)

______________________ ______________________ (Seller)

The Art of Closing Low or No Money Down Deals

Some of the best deals I have found have come through the little classified ad I frequently run in the newspaper. Third Street is one of them. A fellow named Bill called one day and told me he had a six unit building he wanted to sell. He didn't want any Realtors involved, and since he saw my ad he thought I might be interested. I took some of the information down and made an appointment for Dan and I to go see it the following Saturday.

When we got there, I was pleased. There were actually two buildings. One had four units and the other had two units. They were in nice shape, but still needed some minimal cosmetic repair to bring them up to full value. The other pleasant surprise was that this property abutted a seven unit building I owned on Second Street. They were actually back to back with abutting property lines. Owning both of these would give us close to an acre of land in the downtown area! This is quite a holding for any investor. Bill was looking for about $85,000, with $15,000 down.

That asking price was somewhat low (in relation to market value) for six units, but I had bought the seven unit behind it for only $75,000. It was an excellent deal, but it was hard for me to pay more for a building with one less unit in the same neighborhood. Bill took us through the property and we casually mentioned all of the worst points, as usual. Also, we talked to Bill about what he did for a living where he lived, and why he was selling.

We found out that Bill and his wife were school teachers. Bill also had a little saw sharpening business he enjoyed running on the weekends. To drive all the way out to the property because of tenant complaints and spend time on the upkeep was just too much for him. After working all day long, he wanted to relax at home and do some other things besides wasting time on the six-unit.

Sound motivated to you? We learned all we could about Bill's situation. We thought Bill was subtly asking us to buy the six-unit, and we could sense his motivation. What did we do?

Here's another little tidbit of information about negotiating with any seller. It is given in almost every "how to" real estate book I've ever read. They all say, "Don't show your anxiousness to the seller." Let me take that a step further by showing you how we dealt with Bill. That will lead us into the philosophy of what is called "negative selling."

After the tour of the property and our questions to Bill about his life, we were ready to leave. Bill wanted to engage us in more conversation, though. He wanted to learn how interested we were in buying the property. He asked us what we thought about it and whether or not we would make an offer.

Many people (I can hear them now) would show two or three cards in their poker hand right there. They might show their interest, or might give an affirmative about making an offer. Some might even want to make the offer right there, out of excitement. All of these moves would be mistakes.

Here's where we left it, even though we were extremely interested in making the offer. First we said, "Bill, the building is not really bad. However, the price might be a little too high for us." (It sounds like it's my fault, not his. Remember, we don't want to insult the seller blatantly. We want to do it very subtly. The subtle insult we refer to as "THE BLADE.")

"Bill, do you know what I paid for the seven unit right behind your building?" Of course, he says no. I then explain the price and terms. He is surprised, but I don't want to make him look stupid, so now I have to let up and give him an out. I say, "Well, Bill, we did get a very good deal on that, and I'm not saying your building is not worth the price. Actually, Bill, I'm just saying the price might be a little high for us. You see, if we can't get a little positive cash flow, it won't work. It really doesn't make sense for us to buy that way. Of course, you do understand all that, don't you?" (With an open-ended question like that, his answer must be positive. I leave him no choice but to agree with me. I save his dignity, but get my point across, strongly.)

Here's how we wind it up. "Bill, we will have to go put the numbers together and see if there is any way at all we can make it work. If so, we would definitely like to help you out by taking the building off of your hands. If we can't, I will certainly call you and let you know. Is that fair enough?" Now, there's another open ended question. Could Bill possibly reply, "No, Russ, that's not fair?" Of course not. He has to say yes. Does it make sense that if a fellow (seller) is in agreement on many of your small points, he's more apt to agree when we get to the bottom line? Again, there's only one answer, and it does work, doesn't it? I'm glad you agree!

In essence, we had told Bill we would put the numbers together and if they worked we would present an offer. Of course, we knew all along that we would make an offer. What we are doing here is "negative selling." Bill wants to sell and we can feel it. We are very subtly, psychologically, taking that opportunity away from him. Can you feel it?

We also indicated to Bill that we have received dozens of calls on the ad from the paper. We told him we would try to get to his property quickly, but asked him to please be patient. Again, we make it seem that this opportunity could slip away from him. Always plead a very busy schedule. Don't ever let the seller think his deal is the only one you have going. Maintain a confident attitude about your investment formulas and management ability.

It is never a good idea to deal right there, from the hip. As in the case of meeting with the banker, you should prepare a presentation and an offer in writing, never orally. You should go over the entire meeting ahead of time. Put yourself in the seller's shoes and write down every question or objection you think he might have. Prepare an answer or justification for each. If you have a logical reason for each point and use open-ended questions after your explanation of each, it will be hard for him to disagree. By preparing ahead of time you have the distinct advantage, again, of already having been at this meeting once. The second one should come off without a hitch!

The Psychology of Negotiating Offers

Before I explain the rest of our dealings with Bill, I would like to dig deeper into this concept and psychology of negotiating your deals. It is my belief that if you incorporate the psychology of sales (which is, basically, negotiating) into the formulas of real estate investing, your chances of achieving success are much greater.

I have tried to illustrate many of my sales tactics, and show how I use them to close deals, on my terms, throughout this whole book. Each story, starting from the first sale, describes just about every seller; his attitude, his background, his job, his home life, his wants and needs. But you can't just start badgering a guy you don't even know with a million personal questions. If you do, it sounds phony and you both feel uncomfortable. If that happens, chances are there will be no deal.

You have to lead into these questions with casual conversation. I have done it and practiced it so many times, it has become almost second nature to me. If you go back and re-read some of the transactions, you will see exactly how I did it. Every seller is a different person. Every deal is different, as are the terms and circumstances. I have given you some insight on dealing with quite a few types of people.

How I can categorize people, you may ask? It's easy, if you think about it. There are exceptions to the rule, but in general the following procedures work.

The Logic and Reason that Closes the Seller On Your Terms

After you have found a property, worked the numbers and are going to go see it, **"the tour"** begins. You will now be meeting the seller. It is imperative to get the percentages with you. Many books say that investing in real estate is a numbers game, and that's true. However, if you refine your tactics and know how to deal, you can substantially raise the percentages of your success ratio.

"The tour" starts with meeting the seller. The initial meeting, usually at the property, starts with what I call the **"identification period."** The **ID period** is where you must get the seller to like you. You must, in casual conversation, find out the type of work he does. Why? Would you talk to a doctor the same way you would talk to an auto mechanic? Of course not! You need to get on his level and adjust your conversation to his.

Many times a seller will meet you on Saturday to see his property. He may be in jeans and a t-shirt on his day off. He might look like a dump truck driver and be a lawyer, so be careful. Ask questions such as "Do you live around here?" He'll say, "No, I live in Riverdale." "Oh, that's a nice residential area," you reply. "Do you have some children?"

Of course, he's proud of his children, so you've broken the ice and now you're talking. It's natural to just keep asking "off the cuff" questions. Tell him something about yourself. I tell him I have two children, also. "Kids are amazing, aren't they?" I ask. (another open-ended question) You talk on and on, as you go through the property taking notes on the pad you always bring.

After you've collected your data and you've seen the property, leave things up in the air. **"Negative sell"** your interest a little bit, but don't daunt the seller. Be ultra-professional. You are, at this time, preparing them for an offer less than they expect. If you handle the seller the way we handled Bill, the seller will unconsciously know and accept it. Even though you haven't actually said so, the intimation is planted.

The initial ID. period is over. You go home and work up your offer. You then put yourself in the seller's shoes and answer every objection or question you think he'll have. If you "ID'ed" with him properly, you can guess what type of person he is and how he'll react to the low offer. Do you see the purpose for the in-depth initial ID period? It helps you pave the way for the presentation of the offer.

Next comes the phone call to Mr. Seller. Ring, ring, "Mr. Seller, I was able to work up an offer on your property. Is there a particular time that would be best for you, your wife and I to meet?" Don't ever forget to include the spouse, especially on small unit purchases. When you make your presentation you must also divert eye contact to include them. If you don't, they can blow the deal on you quick!

Women can be very influential in the final decision. It's been my experience that the women are usually the ones who pay the bills and handle the checkbooks. The husband portrays the head of the household, but his wife usually controls the budget!

When making the call to schedule an appointment for the presentation, you will inevitably get the hot-shot, superstar seller. He'll ask, "What's the offer? You might as well tell me now, because if it's not what I want you're just wasting your time." He'll carry on with all these tough, superficial reasons why you should tell him your offer over the phone. DON'T EVER DO IT! Simply say, "Mr. Seller, my offer is a bit complicated. I think it would be best for us to discuss it in person. What is the best time for you folks?" Leave it with that open-ended question. Don't let him knock you off guard with the bold approach.

This may surprise you, but the guy who acts bold is usually a cinch to sell. That's exactly why he acts that way. He knows he's easy, so he tries to defend himself up front, before you get a shot at him. He's actually scared to death of getting sold! If you look in his closet when you get to the house, you'll probably find three or four vacuum cleaners, four sets of encyclopedias, a box full of Avon products and 32 million dollars worth of whole life insurance! No wonder he's scared.

Every salesman in town is on a first name basis with him. Stand your ground!

Whether or not you get the bold seller, you now have called and made the appointment for the offer presentation. You arrive exactly on time, as any professional would. You are well groomed, you've gone over all of the questions and objections and you're ready. Now comes the second ID period. You again converse with the seller, whom you have already met, and now with his wife. Keep your eyes open for the usual trophies, plaques and pictures around the house. Try to find a common area of interest.

Continue chatting until they ask about the offer, or you feel that it's time to present it. At that time, you give the wife a copy of the offer, the husband a copy, and keep one copy of the offer for yourself. I will usually let them read the offer before I give any explanation. Sometimes there are no questions at all. Other times they are aghast at the low offer. Either way, I try to show little or no emotion at all. Each offer varies, but I always have a logical and reasonable explanation for the structure of the offer. This describes the offer to Bill and his wife for the six-unit on Third Street. This is **"the presentation"** part of **"the tour,"** after the ID period.

Before I get into the details of **"the presentation,"** let me complete the format with the next to last step, the **"trial close."** If they have many objections to the offer, this can get complicated. If there is only one objection, it is a little easier. For example, let's say they object to the low interest rate you are offering. You must make sure that is the only objection. If it is, you are very close to a deal. The way you do this is by clarifying the objection and then eliminating any and all other objections, as follows:

Clarify the objection. Repeat it to them. "Mr. Seller, if I understand you correctly, you feel that 1-1/2% is too low for the next 30 years." He says, "Absolutely! "

Eliminate all other objections. "If we could agree on a suitable interest rate, would we be in agreement on the rest of the offer?" you ask. If he agrees, then he accepts your purchase price, down payment, closing date, the entire package. Now all you have to work on is the interest rate, and you have a deal.

Any variation works the same way. Eliminate the other objections and negotiate whatever is left.

It is always my policy to assume that they want the deal, unless they absolutely, emphatically say "no." A good way to start closing the offer is to ask them if the closing date is suitable for them. If they say, "yes," start signing the contract.

"The close" is the bottom line, making or breaking the deal. Always have your deposit check (earnest money) written and ready. My usual deposit is $100. I will put the check out on the table with the offer. I use comparable sales in the area, the bad economy and anything else I think they want to hear to justify my offer. The bottom line is to close the deal. Don't make the mistake of being anxious.

Summary:

I) ID period—at the property
2) ID period—before the presentation
3) Presentation
4) Trial Close
5) Final Close

You can refine the steps to fit your own personality. Just remember, all of the steps are necessary to increase the percentage of offers that turn into purchases. Following this format also gives you a chronological order of events so you always know where you are in the negotiating process.

Caution—Never backtrack in the sequence. Never go backwards from the presentation or close to the ID period. After the ID period, the friendship is over. It's now all business. If you backtrack, you lose ground. Don't let them shake you up with objections. Expect objections. If you're offering low, expect them to make you justify it. If you can, you win. If you stumble, you lose.

The Refined Presentation

Now I want you to pay particularly close attention to **"the tour"** with Bill and his wife. You already know the events leading up to the final hour. When we last left Bill we had told him that we would let him know one way or the other about an offer. I want you to pay very close attention to this. It is not often that you will find a building in good repair and negotiate a sale for $2000 less than the owner paid for it three years earlier! Not only that, but for 70% less of a down payment than he paid, too!

I called Bill and told him I had prepared an offer. That same night, after a few rounds of racquetball, Dan and I were going to meet the owner/broker to negotiate the Spanish mansion purchase. Since we would be at the broker's office, I asked him if we could use the conference room for this negotiation, also. He said it would be fine. I had Bill and his wife scheduled for 8:30 p.m. We met the owner of the Spanish mansion at 7:00 p.m. At 8:30 p.m., we were still negotiating when Bill and his wife arrived. We decided Dan would finish up on the "Spanish mansion" contract and I would take Bill and his wife to another office.

Bill introduced me to his wife and we sat and chatted for awhile. She was a school teacher, too, and had some unique stories to tell. After awhile I decided it was time for **"the presentation".** I opened my briefcase and handed each of them a copy of the offer. The offer I had written was for $74,000, with $7,500 down. I had scheduled a closing date for the 4th of April. By doing that I would get the benefit of the prorated rents and securities. At closing, it would cost us only $5,500 to own the six unit.

How Pro-rations Can Make You Big Money at the Closing

For those of you who are familiar with pro-rations, let me explain. Any time you buy a multi-unit building with rent payments due on the first, schedule your closing for the third or fourth of the month. The seller will be responsible to collect the rents on the first, but he is only entitled to keep those few days of it. At closing, he must pay you the rent due for the 26 or 27 days you will own the building.

Example:

1) Rents for month total $1,500

2) Seller collects $1,500 on the first of the month

3) Seller sells building to you on the 4th

4) $1,500 divided by 30 days in month equals $50 per day.

5) You will own the building from the 4th to the 30th , a total of 26 days.

6) 26 days x $50 = $1,300

7) At closing, $1,300 will be deducted from your down payment.

It's a pretty neat trick, isn't it? Let's continue our negotiations. My offer was $74,000 with $7,500 down and the following terms. I would be purchasing "subject to" (similar to assuming)

1. The first mortgage of $15,000 at 7-1/2%
2. The second mortgage of $11,111 at 8-1/2 %
3. The third mortgage of $16,898 at 10%
4. The fourth mortgage of $12,571 at 10%
5. Sellers to hold a fifth mortgage at $10,895 at 11% for 20 years.

Can you believe those low interest mortgages? The beauty of this deal is that all of those mortgages will be paid off in 1989. They are all into principal and the sellers don't even know it! I will, when this deal goes through, own a building worth over $100,000 with less than $10,000 owed on it in six years.

"The presentation": Bill and his wife were silent as they read the offer. I spoke first and said, "Bill, I am actually offering you $78,000, not $74,000. The reason we offered it this way is quite simple. There wasn't room on the offer to write it all, so I thought I would just explain it when we got together. You told me you would like to get $80,000-$85,000 for your property. If it was listed with a Realtor, there would be a 10% commission, or $8,000. This means you have to get $15 ,000 down to net the same $7,500 down I am offering. In this market that might be pretty difficult to do, wouldn't you agree?" (Open ended question, to which he has to agree)

"Also, if it was listed at around $80,000 or $85,000, you are probably going to get offers around $78,000 anyway. Nobody ever wants to pay full price. So what we did, in essence, is this. We have overhead for ads, our office, a phone, and so forth. Considering the fact that you only called two days ago and I'm here today to help you, that's a quick sale. I think we could agree that if you listed with a Realtor, it could take six months, or even a year to sell your property. So we took a sale price of $78,000, which is a realistic price, then deducted $8,000 which a Realtor would deduct from his commission. This leaves a price of $70,000. We split the commission in half with you and your wife. We added $4,000 to the sale price making it $74,000. We gave ourselves a credit for the other $4,000. I don't think we could be more fair than that, do you?"

They sat and thought about it for quite a while. I did not say a word. Bill broke the silence and asked if this was our best offer. I could read in his face he didn't want to lose us, but his ego forced him to make an attempt at negotiating. Not wanting to lose the deal, but also not wanting to go any higher, I had to do two things. I had to bluff Bill into thinking this was our best offer. I also had to do it with extreme subtleness. I did not want to put his ego in jeopardy, nor did I want to embarrass him or his wife. My reply had to appeal to his sense of fair play and I had to close on that note. I said, "Bill, I think we've been very fair with the offer. We could have come in with a much lower offer, haggled and played games with you. I felt that you were beyond that and would probably be insulted with that type of game. We have gone over the numbers very carefully and tried to structure as fair an offer as we could. You are a school teacher and have an extensive educational background. (Stroke his ego a little—make him feel good.) I am confident that you understand we have guidelines to follow in investing. I never tell a seller, 'This is my bottom line, take it or leave it.' It would be quite unfair of me to take that type of stand. I'm only saying we tried to be as fair as possible, without making a bad investment for ourselves." Then, I shut up and didn't say another word. I am so sincere in my bluff, and so honest that it is tough to combat me. If I have built rapport with this seller and he likes me, an honest, sincere approach will knock the wind right out of his sails. It works if you're prepared, ahead of time, to deal with your seller. Also, if you'll notice, I never did answer his question.

The next minor objection came from his wife. She asked if they had to make a decision right then. This is probably the objection every salesman in the world hates. It is also the most popular. "I want to think about it." Well, there are many techniques to get around that in sales, but real estate is a little different. Also, since the Mrs. asked the question, I had to be careful. She was testing our honest approach. If we were so sincere, then there should be no reason they couldn't at least take the night to sleep on it. After all, this was a major decision. It was their first attempt at selling income property, and $74,000 would be a big decision.

My instincts as a salesman go against this type of thinking. I want to close, right now. I have been brainwashed in sales on certain points. One is, if you don't close them right there, they won't buy. They will find a million reasons they shouldn't buy, whether the reasons are valid or not.

Real estate is a little different. I felt if I pressured them for a commitment now, they would think they were being wheeled. Nonetheless, I planted the seed for a fairly quick decision, so as not to be strung along. You will run into these types of people when you start investing. Here's how I answered.

"No, I don't think you have to make a decision right now. (This drops her guard.) How do you feel about the offer, though? Are there any questions about it?" She said she didn't have any. "Well," I said, "I don't want to go too long, because we are involved with quite a few projects now and we do need to know where to allocate our monies." At that, they agreed to get in touch the following day with their decision. We parted on a warm and positive note.

I usually like to go to the county courthouse and look up the documentary stamps on a property before I make an offer. The documentary stamps will tell you what the sellers paid for the property and when they bought it. If you go to your county courthouse, the people who work there will usually be very helpful in showing you how to do this. I didn't do that in this case and I'm glad I didn't.

If I had researched the documentary stamps, I would have found that Bill and his wife had paid $76,000 for the property three years earlier. I don't ever remember offering anyone (knowingly) less money than they actually paid for a property! If I had known ahead of time, I very well might have offered them quite a bit more than $74,000!

They called me the next day and asked me to come out to their house so we could all sign the contracts and expedite a closing. I still don't know what to attribute this success to, except the logic and reason used in the presentation.

The same holds true for the duplexes I purchased for no money down from Mr. Carter. If you have a logical reason for the offer you've structured, your chances for getting it accepted are much better. Don't just flail away. Prepare ahead of time. Practice your "tour!"

The following page is a copy of the signed offer on Bill's property.

SALES CONTRACT

Sanibel, Florida 3/11 19 83

Receipt is hereby acknowledged by the undersigned [redacted] of the sum of one hundred dollars

~~illiam Clausen and any other legal owner hereunder~~ Dollars ($ 100.00)

from Darell A. Whitney and Daniel [illegible] Kelly

as a deposit on account of the purchase price of the following described property upon the terms and conditions as stated herein. Said deposit, and any further deposits received on this transaction to be held in [redacted] compliance with Florida Real Estate Law.

Description of Property, same being in Lee County, Florida

~~2553 Laird Street, Ft. Myers, Fla. Legal description, as per deed.~~

Purchase Price: [illegible] FOUR THOUSAND Dollars ($ 74,000.00)

Terms and conditions of sale: Buyers agree to purchase subject to the following mortgages.

1. 1st - [illegible]5,025.00 7.5% and payment approx. $175.00 per month. Paid in 199[illegible].
2. 2nd - [illegible].00 8.5% and " " [illegible]90.00 " " " 1989.
3. 3rd - 6,808.00 10 % and " " [illegible]04.00 " "
4. 4th - [illegible],571.00 [illegible].5 " " [illegible] " "
5. Buyers to give back a 5th mortgage to sellers for [illegible]0,695.00 [illegible]
6. Buyers will pay $7,500.00 in a down payment (cash, certified check).

Seller warrants that there are $800.00 in security deposits. Seller also warrants that all plumbing, electrical and appliances will be in working order upon closing. Seller agrees to provide buyers with a list of all furnishings and any other items that will be included in the sale. Seller will also provide buyers with [illegible] last year['s] [illegible] service bills, (except water & sewer) utilities [illegible] insurance, [illegible] warrant the accuracy of same. (8) Sellers will pay ½ of title insurance

1. **ACCEPTANCE:** If this offer is not accepted by the seller on or before presentation, the aforesaid deposit monies shall be, at the option of the buyer, returned to him, and this agreement shall be null and void.

2. **EVIDENCE OF TITLE:** Seller shall furnish, at his expense, an up-to-date abstract XXXXXXXX or apply $ [illegible] toward the total cost of title insurance. In the event title is not found to be good, marketable and insurable, all monies paid by the buyer shall be returned, and the parties hereto shall be released from all obligations; or, buyer may accept title as is.

3. **CONVEYANCE:** Seller shall convey the aforesaid property to the buyer by General Warranty Deed.

4. **RESTRICTIONS AND EASEMENTS:** It is understood and agreed that this property is being sold and purchased subject to the restrictions and limitations of record common to the neighborhood, and subject to any assessments for public utilites which may be of record. Furthermore, it is understood and agreed that this property is being sold and purchased subject to the approval of a percolation and soilanalysis. If sanitary sewerage is not available to the property, at the seller's expense. Furthermore, seller must furnish on any building an affirmative test that no wood boring insects exist and there is no damage existing from previous infestations.

5. **PRORATIONS:** Insurance, interest, rents and other expenses or revenues of said property shall be prorated as of the date of closing. Taxes and other assessments shall be prorated as of the date of closing on the basis of the last assessment records available.

6. **APPLIANCES:** All electrical, mechanical and gas appliances shall be in working condition at date of closing, normal wear and tear excepted.

7. **CLOSING DATE:** This transaction shall be closed and the buyer shall pay the balance of the monies and execute all papers necessary for the completion of his purchase on or before 4/4/83, otherwise, the deposit monies paid this date shall be retained by the seller or agent as liquidated and agreed damages, and the parties hereto shall be released from all obligations under this instrument.

8. **POSSESSION** will be given on or before 4/4/83 [illegible]

9. **RISK:** Until delivery of the deed, the risk of loss or damage to said property is assumed by the seller.

10. **THIS** contract shall be binding upon the parties hereto, their respective heirs, executors and assigns.

11. **SELLER'S EXPENSES:** Seller is to pay the following: (a) cost of furnishing complete Abstract of title certified to date (and also current chattel search if personal property is included as part of the above described property); (b) preparation of warranty deed and deed stamps; (c) mortgage intangible tax and recording fee for any purchase-money mortgage to seller; (d) real estate Brokerage fee; (e) special taxes or assessments for which a bill has been rendered, on or before the date of the acceptance of this contract; (f) condominium transfer fee, if any.

12. **BUYER'S EXPENSES:** Buyer is to pay for the following: (a) recording fee for warranty deed; (b) preparation of note and mortgage, and note stamps on note, for any purchase-money mortgage, or any costs of any institutional loan secured by Buyer; (c) mortgage transfer fee, if required; (d) cost of survey, if required; (e) recording of Approval for Membership, if applicable; (f) special taxes or assessment for which no bill has been rendered, on or before the date of the acceptance of this contract.

13. **PRO-RATIONS:** The following items will be pro-rated at closing, as of the closing date (a) real estate taxes (b) interest on any assumed indebtedness; (c) insurance, unless Buyer elects to take out new insurance; (d) rent; (e) condominium maintenance, if applicable.

14. **ASSIGNABILITY:** (check one) Buyer ☒ May assign ☐ May-not assign, contract

[redacted] By ____________________

I, or we, agree to purchase the above described property on the terms and conditions stated in the above instrument.

Witness: Purchaser Date ____________

____________________ ( ) ____________________ (Seal)

____________________ ( ) ____________________ (Seal)

I, or we, agree to sell the above described property to the above named purchaser on the terms and conditions stated in the above instrument.

Witness: Seller Date 3/11/83

____________________ ( ) [signature] (Seal)

____________________ ( ) M. Katherine Clausen (Seal)

Understand the Game by Knowing the Pitfalls

Now I would like to give you some insight into the game you are about to enter. Real estate investing can be a wonderful, fulfilling and self-satisfying business. It can also be nerve-racking if you don't understand the how's and why's of what makes it work or not work. It is important that you understand the fundamental laws.

Law I

This is the "law of use." It simply says, *"Whatever you don't use, you lose."* That means if you tie your arm to your body, and leave it there long enough, you'll never use it again! The only way to keep your arm is to keep using it. The same thing goes for your brain. It is important to remind yourself of this often. In fact, this applies to all human virtues. Ambition, unused, tends to diminish and disappear. The same is true for courage. Unused, it deteriorates and withers away. Compassion, excitement, or ingenuity, all behave in the same manner. Here's what it pays to do. Take inventory constantly of everything you possess in the way of talents, activity, energy, a positive attitude, and brain power. Make sure it is being used every day. And remember that key phrase, *"If you quit, you lose."*

Law II

The second law is "the law of averages." The "law of averages" says that if you do something often enough, you will get what is called a "ratio of results." The key to understanding this law is that *it will work for anybody who wants to try it!*

Even a child can do it. Send a small child out with some bars of soap. Tell him to knock on every door on the block, and when someone answers the door say, "I've got the finest soap made to sell. Would you like to buy some?" Even if a little 8 year old child knocks on enough doors, someone will buy!

And if you knock on enough doors, someone will buy from you, too. If you put in enough low offers on income properties, someone will accept! Some people won't be home, some won't want to be disturbed, some already have plenty of what you've got. But sure enough, if you knock on enough doors, someone will buy. The same thing that works in sales, works for income property. If you run ads in the classified section, use a Realtor, and pass out business cards, sooner or later you will kick up a property with which to get your feet wet. A ratio will develop for anybody that is willing to try.

People will read my book, as they will read others. There is enough information here to move anyone off center. Some people will read this book and be ready to take the world apart, but they will never buy their first property. Why? Because even though they finally have some ideas and a good vehicle, they let the little things interfere. That's called *"the language of the poor"*.

People have the most amazing ability to major in minor things. Learn not to do that! Learn to do the major things first, and most times the minor things take care of themselves. Turn your life around on that score. Some people let all of their time get eaten up, and the little plant that could become a money tree gets choked to death by little things.

Law III

The *"Law of Sowing and Reaping."* For most of my life I didn't understand much of sowing and reaping. I was too busy trying to find the money to pay the bills. Here's what the law says: *"Whatever a man sows, he reaps."* Sounds simple, doesn't it? Let me also add this. Many points I'm discussing are not up for a majority vote. They are sound. If you sow well, you reap well. My interpretation is, if you plant pumpkin seed, you won't get thistles. Mother Nature won't pull tricks on you. Anyone can tell how things are going to turn out if he plans with intelligence. Learn how to invest yourself. Learn to invest your excitement. Learn to invest your natural talents, your compassion and vitality. Most important, learn to invest your time wisely. That's how you guarantee a better harvest.

Now if you want to become wealthy, the key word to wealth is. . . .people. Invest in other people. The Master Teacher said two thousand years ago, "If a man wishes to be great at anything, let him find a way to become a servant of many people." You see, people are where the wealth is. Inevitably some reader will say, "Not me. I can't be responsible for half the community. About the best I can do is take care of myself." Friends, that's a poor man talking.

Control of Your Thinking

Here's where you can really get going or get in trouble. It's the way you think. One fellow says, "It's not my drinking that's got me stinking. It's my stinking thinking that's got me drinking!" That is exactly what can happen. There is an Old Testament phrase that says it pretty well. "As a man thinketh in his heart, so is he."

A man's conversation is the product of the way he thinks. What he wears, what he drives, where he lives, how much he earns: the sum total of a man's life is the product of the way he thinks.

The quality of a man's conversation is the product of what gets poured into his brain. The fabric of a man's life is built from those ingredients poured into his mental factory.

That is what you must learn to do first. Start substituting the positive for the negative. Throw out the trash. You cannot build a dynamic prosperous, happy and fulfilling life with ingredients from a garbage can. Start making a deliberate attempt to talk about the good things. Read the good books, listen to good music. Don't waste your time dwelling on problems. Spend most of the time on finding solutions. I'm not saying you can become 100% positive, but the better the ratio of positive to negative, the easier it is to change the fabric of your economic, social, and personal life.

Setting Goals

What about setting goals? Almost everyone has heard the phrase. Just about every success book you read talks about goals. Most successful people attribute their success to their ability to set goals. Is this just corny rhetoric or is there something to this?

I think goal setting is one of the most important attributes to success. How can a man be successful in anything unless he picks a direction? But it isn't always easy to know where you're headed. It takes labor, sweat and toil, which is why a lot of people don't bother. Many people work hard on their jobs, but not on their future.

First of all, you have to set your sights high. Make it important and work on it until it becomes a strong desire. Make your life more exciting and adventurous by doing this daily. Work on your goals and develop what you want. It's not important to win all the time, either.

The best baseball players in history (their names are in the Hall of Fame) batted a 400 average.

Do you know what 400 is for a lifetime average? This means that during their careers, six times out of every ten that they got up to bat, they STRUCK OUT. I'll tell you something about a champion, though. He might be out, but he's not through. You don't have to hit a home run every time. Babe Ruth used to go up to the plate, strike out and on his way back to the dug out have a big grin on his face. They used to say, "Babe, how come you're smiling? You just struck out!" Babe would say, "I'm that much closer to my next home run." That's what's important. Not winning every time, but playing every time. In fact, it's not important to get everything you want, but you have to want everything you get. Set it up and go for it.

Here are two things to get your life started in a new direction. Set up a game plan. Set up something to go for and think you're going to win everything. Then play your heart out.

Chapter V

Reference Section

Summary

Perhaps many people just getting started are having the same problem that I was. I was very eager to start investing, but there were times when I felt I wasn't moving fast enough towards my goal.

It's very important that you budget your time wisely. You've got to make every minute count. For this reason, I thought it would be helpful for you to see how my schedule goes on an average day.

Monday

1) 5:30 a.m.—Wake up

2) Have coffee and read paper (check classified for new ads);

3) 6:00 a.m.—in my office, at home, organizing the day, checking calendar for any appointments;

4) 6:30 a.m.—write in my book, read some new literature, or listen to some tapes on attitude, motivation, or real estate (feed the mind daily);

5) 7:30-8:00 a.m.—Start making calls, either on properties found in classifieds, or return calls from people who called me on my "investor ad";

6) 9:00 a.m.-5:00 p.m. — Out in the field, either looking at properties, checking with Realtors, making offers, checking on a rehab or painter (if we're involved in a fixer-upper at that time); in general, out seeing the people all day.

Hint: I always carry a pad and pencil for drive-bys. These are properties you just happen to drive past and see that they are neglected. Look for an overgrown lawn, dirty windows, or the exterior needing paint. I am always on the lookout for anything in disrepair. I take down the address and look up the owner's address at the County Courthouse. We will usually write a letter first and ask if he is interested in selling. If no response is received within a week, I will follow up with a phone call.

7) 10:00-11:00 p.m.—Bedtime. My daily schedule doesn't vary much most days of the week. Of course, I set time aside for the children and my wife. I also schedule several hours about three or four days of the week for tennis, racquetball or some type of exercise. These revolve around business, though, which is the priority.

I realize that not everyone likes to get up at 5:00 a.m. I don't mean to say that this is a criterion for success. It is not. I just happen to like the early morning hours best. It is peaceful at that time of the day. The phones aren't ringing, and there are no interruptions. This is my time to think, plan and organize. I personally am extremely effective at that time. I do not condone sleeping until 8:00 or 9:00 every day, either. This is lazy! Saturday and Sundays are sometimes full business days. Real estate investing is unique that way. Sometimes Tuesday or Friday can be a slack day for business, whereas Saturday will be extremely busy. When you've got your own business, every day is Saturday.

Techniques for Locating Properties

1. Classified ads (especially under income property for sale)
2. Drive-bys
3. Realtors
4. Code Enforcement Bureau of your local City Hall. With this technique, you simply go to the Code Enforcement Bureau and ask for a list of the condemned properties or properties with building code violations. Contact the owners either by mail or phone and ask them if they want to sell their property. Remember, it's a numbers game. Everyone of them that says no gets you that much closer to the one who will say yes. Don't let a little rejection stop you. Go for it until you get one. Make that a goal.
5. Legal Notice section of your local paper. This usually precedes the classified section and lists properties which are being foreclosed upon or seized by the IRS and auctioned off. My book on how to buy at foreclosure, "The Great American Land Rush," tells you where to

locate the properties, and how to buy them. This is a very lucrative market now. Foreclosures are at their highest rate since the Depression. Approximately one out of every 200 mortgages are currently being foreclosed. Ask your banker and/or mortgage broker about any foreclosures or special assets they may have.

6. FHA/VA Repossessions — Write to your local HUD office and Veterans Administration and ask to be put on the mailing list for these properties. You can also check through your Realtor. These properties, in many instances, can be picked up with 100% financing or very low down payments.

7. Run your own classified ad. I've saved the best for last. This has been my best source for picking up excellent bargain properties. Recently, there was a real estate seminar in this area. It was one of those get rich quick seminars and I saw five or six ads in the paper the following week. After that I never saw another one. I called a few of them just for the heck of it to see how these people handled the calls. I was not surprised that they had discontinued their ads. They lacked professionalism, and didn't even seem to know what type of information to ask the caller. I will go into detail on what to say when answering the phone. First, here is the "gold mine ad."

Run under: Income Property For Sale or Real Estate Wanted

"An Investor wants to buy income property.
Will look at all, any condition."

You will not believe the response! My phone rings off the hook when I run that ad. All types of property owners will call—single family owners, duplex owners, motel owners, commercial property owners, or big multi-unit owners. I used to run that ad in New York and I still run it here in Florida. It has worked well in both states, I'm sure it will work for you.

The ads I saw after the flunky seminar ran along these lines: "I will buy your house, if you sell for no money down," or "I buy houses if your terms are flexible."

I'm sure they work to some extent, but they lack the professionalism of the investor ad. Also, as I said, when I called those ads and told them I had a property to sell, they did not know what to ask or how to proceed. If you're not professional and have to grope for words, you will scare the bargain property seller off.

Working Smarter—Not Harder

Here is a typical call, along with some variations, to give you an idea on what to do when the phone starts ringing.

Caller: "Hello, are you the party whc has the ad in the paper to buy income property?"

Me: "Yes, that is correct!" (Silence—let them talk.)

Caller: "Well, I have a duplex in Fort Myers and I would like to sell it."

Me: "I see. Is it listed with a Realtor?"

*Find this out immediately. The best deals will be the ones not listed. If you get the people to call you to sell their property before it's exposed, that's where you'll generally find your bargain.

Caller: "No, it's not listed. We were thinking about listing it, but we saw your ad and thought we'd see if you would be interested first."

*Always act as if you do this all the time and have plenty of experience. Also, act as if people call you all the time to buy property. If the terms fit your parameters, tell them you will make an offer, usually within a few days.

Me: "Are there any mortgages on the property?"

*Always have a pad and pencil ready to write this information down. This way, at the end of your conversation, you'll know if it's worth pursuing. Keep your ears tuned to their motivation for selling.

Caller: "Yes, we have a first mortgage."

Me: "What is the amount left on the mortgage?"

*You have to know these things to determine if you should pursue the deal. Some callers may be reluctant to give this information. If so, just say, "Sir, need to I know this to determine whether or not your property fits our requirements for purchasing." He'll give you the information if you sound professional, and you'll have his total respect. Remember, he has called you, and is on your turf! Be firm!

Caller: "I owe $32,000."

Me: "At what rate of interest?"

Caller:: "8-1/2 % ."

Me: "And the payment per month?"

Caller: "$ 154"

Me:: "What are the rents?"

*Now you get into rent roll and debt service to determine if you can get some cash flow.

Caller: "$295 for each unit, for a total of $590 per month."

Me: "Are they currently rented?"

Caller: "Yes. "

Me: "What are the taxes?"

Caller: "$600 per year, but they are included in my mortgage payment."

Me: "Who pays the utilities?"

Caller: "The tenants do."

(After I gather the pertinent info.)

Me: "Sir, why are you selling this property?"

*You will get a variety of answers, so probe a little to find out how motivated he really is. The more problems, the better. He will be more motivated then. With the data collected thus far, this looks like a very good property to pursue.

Me: "What type of price are you looking for?"

Caller: "Well, we are looking to get about $49,000."

Me: "Would you consider holding some of the mortgage?"

*You'll get a variety of answers here also. You have to be tuned to the caller. Try to ID with him and find out where his head really is.

Some will say yes, and some will say no. Explain your requirements. Tell him you usually don't go much higher than a 10% down payment, depending on the particular property and circumstances. Tell him you need the seller to hold some of the mortgage. Explain, in today's market, this is the common way to sell. The folks who aren't open-minded aren't selling their properties. They maybe listed, but they certainly aren't selling.

If you get any kind of positive response, continue. If you don't get any positive response and you sense the conversation coming to an end, always thank him for calling and tell him you appreciate his time. Never burn any bridges. If he liked you and respected your professionalism, he may tell a friend about you, or may even call back in the future.

(Assuming there was some positive response, you continue.)

Me: "Sir, I think we may have an interest in your property. What is the street address so we can send our appraiser out to have a look at it?" (An appraiser sounds professional and organized.)

Caller: "2515 2nd Avenue."

Me: "What is your phone number so I can get back in touch to make an offer if we are interested?"

There are many variations, depending on your caller. I hope this little guideline will keep you from stumbling until you gain a little experience. After awhile, you will be able to discount many of the callers from the information gathered on the phone. Until then, I would go meet them all. Remember, I bought the six unit, the two duplexes and several others from sellers calling on that very same ad!

Techniques for Starting Capital

1. Refinance your home (or second mortgage)
2. Home improvement loan
3. Passbook loan
4. Personal loan
5. Loan on a paid-off automobile
6. Borrow from a relative
7. Take on a partner
8. Blanket mortgage or bridging loan
9. Do whatever it takes, just get started!

List of Good Books or Tapes

* * * 1. Financial Genius—*Mark O. Haroldsen*

* * 2. Real Estate Money Machine— *Wade Cook*

* * 3. How to Master Your Financial Destiny—*Mark O. Haroldsen*

* 4. How to Use Leverage to Make Money in Local Real Estate—*George Bockl*

5. Complete Guide to Real Estate Financing—*Jack Cummings*

* * 6. Financial Freedom Report—*National Institute of Financial Planning*

7. You Can Negotiate Anything—*Herb Cohen* * * *

8. The Closers — *William 8L Stephen Publishing*

* 9. Two Years for Freedom—*Bill Greene*

10. Think and Grow Rich—*Napoleon Hill*

* 11. Psychology of Winning—*Denis Waitley*

12. How To Master The Art of Selling Anything—*Tom Hopkins*

13. Real Estate Exchange and Acquisition Techniques—*William Tappan*
14. Real Estate Turnaround—*Craig Hall*
15. Financial Genius Tapes — *Mark* 0. *Haroldsen*
16. How to Get Government Loans *Wayne Phillips*

I would start with the books and tapes beside the asterisks. After you've read several, you'll be knowledgeable enough to decide what others would be of benefit to you.

Formulas—Rules for Negotiating

1) Don't show anxiousness.
2) Find out all you can about the seller.
3) Find out how long he's owned the property.
4) Why is he selling?
5) How much did he paid for the property? (Check documentary stamps at county courthouse.)

What to Let the Seller Know

1) All little things wrong with the property (either directly or indirectly through Realtor.)
2) You have a busy schedule.
3) About other properties you may own
4) Examples of some of the good purchases you've made
5) Some information about yourself and your family
6) Your excellent management history and ability
7) Your tough buying criteria (be realistic)

Find Out More Information

1) Is he the decision maker (or is his wife)?
2) Where does he work?
3) How many children does he have?
4) Where does he live?
5) What are his likes, dislikes, hobbies, interests?

For the Bank

1) Put it on paper—(always)
A. Description of property
B. Glossy pictures (before and after)
C. Portfolio of other properties owned
D. Present rent roll, projected rent roll and debt service statement
2. Be professional and confident
3. Be well-dressed and groomed
4. Be prepared

Realtor Criteria

1. He should be ambitious and work full-time.

2. Try to find a rookie (they are easier to mold and more ambitious).

3. Your Realtor should work for you.

4. Inform him of your tough criteria and methods—you are a "serious buyer."

Returns on Cash Invested

1) Calculate cash investment (down payment for a 30-50% return in first year)

A) Out of pocket money in investment

B) How much in your pocket in one year (Example—If you put $5,000 down and return $2,000 net [in one year] your return is 40%.)

C) $2,000 divided by $5,000 = 40%

D) If the numbers don't work, don't make the investment

2. How to put it on paper (Example—4 units):

A) Rents Unit one: $275.00
Unit two: $230.00
Unit three $230.00
Unit four $220.00
Total rents per month $955.00 or $11,460 per year

Purchase price: $60,000.00
Down Payment (@ 10%) $ 6,000.00

B. Variable Expenses
1. Taxes: $133.33, or $1,600 per year
2. Insurance: $37.50, or $450.00 per year

3. Utilities: Tenants pay for individual units;
a) $85 monthly for common area electric, or $1,020 per year
4. Miscellaneous Permits: $14.49 monthly or $173.88 per year
C. Mortgages
1) 1st Mortgage (to be assumed) @ $40,000 at 10% APR, Monthly payment $363.49
2) 2nd Mortgage (to seller) at 12% for 10 years, Monthly payment $172.17
D. Rent Pro-ration: (If closing is set for 3rd day of a 30 day month)
1) Rent = $955 per month
2) $955 divided by 30 days = $31.83 per day
3) $31.83 x 27 days = $859.41 (to be deducted from down payment at closing)
4) $6,000 down payment less $859.41=$5,140.59 total down payment

****

Yearly:	Monthly:		
Gross Rents:		$11,460.00	$955.00
Debt Service		6,427.92	535.66
Expenses:		3,243.84	270.32
NOI (Net Operating Income)		$1,788.24	$149.02

*Divide your first year's NOI ($1,788.24) by your net down payment ($5,140.59) and this will give you your percentage of return on cash in the first year (35%).
($1,788.74 divided by $5,140.59 = .34786 or 35%)

This would appear to be a very good deal. If there is room to improve the building and raise rents, you could even show a greater return.

There are some variables to consider when you figure your prorations and bottom line outlay. These costs vary from state to state, so check with your Realtor or title company to find out who is responsible for these costs in your particular state.

Other Costs or Pro-rations Might Include the Following:

1. Title insurance (In Florida, the seller pays it) so that it is a debit to the seller.
2. Documentary stamps (recording fees)
3. Attorney fees (if you use one)
4. Tax pro-ration (In Florida, these are paid in arrears)
5. Assumed insurance pro-rations
6. Interest pro-rations on mortgage
7. Deed surtax (if any)
8. Mortgage transfer fees (if any)
9. State stamps (on mortgage note)
10. Intangible tax (on mortgage note)
11. Updating Abstract (if not using title insurance)
12. Cost for amortization schedule (if any and not included in title insurance)

Several of these costs would probably be included in the cost of the title insurance or the attorney fees. Most are minimal, so don't get caught up by the minor details. First get the main thing done-find a deal!

Sum It Up

Tips for producing good investments with the largest returns and shelters:

1. Income producing property only
2. Leverage (use other people's money)
3. Sound property (financially and structurally)
4. Improve the property (cosmetics—upgrade tenants)
5. Good and careful management
6. Raise rents
7. Sell, trade, refinance, second mortgage or home improvement loan for more cash
8. Repeat process over and over

9. Never try to make a bad investment good by holding on to it.
10. Settle with the failure, alleviate the problem and move on.

Remember—

Many will be the ones who say, "It can't be done." They will be relatives and loved ones. They will be acquaintances, associates, mothers, fathers, sisters and brothers. There will be many. Happy and fulfilled is he that becomes the minority within the majority. Those who stand with him, will reap the benefits of his success, for the approval of others is not his goal.

Hustle

Hustle is doing something that everyone is absolutely, certain can't be done.

Hustle is getting the deal because you got there first, or stayed there after everyone else gave up.

Hustle is shoe leather and elbow grease and sweat and missing lunch.

Hustle is getting the offer accepted after they've said "No" twenty times.

Hustle is believing in yourself and the business you're in.

Hustle is the sheer joy of winning.

Hustle is being the sorest loser in town.

Hustle is hating to take a vacation because you might miss a piece of the action.

Hustle is heaven if you're a hustler.

Hustle is hell if you're not!

Appendix

1. **Contract for Deed (Land Contract)** — This form of financing is generally used when a buyer wishes to utilize or assume the present financing on a property and it is not assumable. There is quite a bit of controversy on this topic so be sure to consult your attorney before entering any agreement.

Your attorney will draw an agreement which gives the buyer all of the benefits of ownership. The title to the property, however, is not transferred to the buyer until the mortgages are satisfied or paid off. (see page 6)

2. **Prorated Rents**—This is explained fully in Chapter IV. It is a technique used by investors to lower the down payment when purchasing an income property. (see page 7)

3. FHA **Title I Home Improvement Loans**—This loan generated over $60,000 for me in my beginning stages of investing. This loan is given by both savings and loans and commercial banks. The money lent is guaranteed to the bank by the federal government, which makes it a very safe loan for the lender. Usually, you can borrow up to $7,500 unsecured or up to $15,000 secured by a lien on your property. The lender presently can charge up to 16% interest for fifteen years or less. One percent is usually charged for the origination fee. I strongly recommend that any investor, who is serious about getting started, investigate this source of seed capital. (see page 9)

4. **Redlining**—Although this is an illegal practice, many lending institutions have areas designated as blighted or declining neighborhoods. They will use other reasons for not lending in the redlined areas and will deny the practice of redlining. (see page 15)

5. **Land Contract**—(see Contract for Deed, page 16)

6. **Interest Only Note**—This is an arrangement between lender and borrower (private or conventional) where the borrower pays interest only on the principal amount owed. Sometime in the future, usually a predetermined date, the principal balance becomes due and payable, in full. (see page 50)

7. **Balloon Payment**—When a mortgage or note is amortized over a number of years to keep the monthly payment low, but sometime before the note matures, the entire balance owed becomes due and payable. My advice is to stay away from balloons if possible. They are promises you may not be able to keep. (see page 50)

8. **Municipal Housing Authority (MHA)**— These are subsidized rents. Most cities have a local office that will pay a portion (percentage) of the rent for people with low or moderate incomes. This is an excellent source of tenants and the MHA portion of the rent arrives every month on the first, directly from Uncle Sam. (see page 58)

9. **Wraparound Mortgage (Wrap)**—This is a form of financing that involves a mortgage which encompasses (or wraps around) other existing mortgages. (see pages 5-7)

Example— I sell a 2 unit property. I have a first and second mortgage on it presently. I am going to hold a third mortgage in addition to the cash down. Instead of holding a separate document in the amount of the third mortgage, I hold a mortgage in the total amount of the existing mortgages plus the amount that would have been the third mortgage. The buyer will make one payment to me and I will pay the other mortgage payments and keep the difference.

10. **Short Term Capital Gain**—This is a tax consequence one must face if he sells his property after owning it for less than one year and one day. He will be taxed on 100% of the profit as opposed to only 40% with a long term capital gain. For further information you should consult with your accountant. (see page 88)

11. **"Subject to"**—This is a legal term in the wording of a contract for purchase. It is similar to "assuming," not encompassing. Consult your attorney for more detailed advice. (see page 102)

FROM THE DESK OF RUSSELL A. WHITNEY

An amazing statistic crossed my desk, and I haven't been able to get it out of my mind. This tragedy, happening all over America, just doesn't seem possible in a society of free enterprise and equal opportunity. With all of the literature that is available on real estate investing and with the quality of *free* seminars that teach the basic techniques of making money in real estate, even to beginners without any cash, I am just amazed that something like this could happen.

Actually, when I sat down and analyzed it, I realized that some of my own relatives come under this same devastating statistic.

Since you have read this far, let me share this terrible reality with you.

91. 6 % of the American public will retire at or below the poverty level.

Do you hear me? Ninety-one point six percent at or below the poverty level at retirement! That, my friend, is an awesome statistic. Less than *10%* of us even have a chance at a decent life after working for practically all our adult lifetimes. We'll still retire poor.

This is a matter of deep personal concern to me, and I want, desperately, for you to understand that statistic for yourself and your family. My father-in-law, who worked for 22 years in a secure union job, just retired a short time ago. After all those years of loyalty, he is now receiving a pension and a social security check which both total approximately $700 per month. That little bit of money barely covers the bills, let alone having any left over for luxuries or fun.

About 15 years ago, my father and mother-in-law purchased the house they still live in for a total of $12,000. Today, it has, obviously, appreciated in value and is worth about $75,000. Isn't that a familiar story? They have finally paid it off so it is now free and clear. They can't sell it because they need a place to live and they don't want to borrow against it because, then, they would have more monthly payments. That, in my opinion, is a crime after someone works all of their life.

Are you going to allow this to be your future?

If I could have convinced my father-in-law, 15 years ago, to just buy *one more* house and let the rent pay for it over the years, he would now have an extra $75,000 nest egg to retire on. That would sure make things a lot different for him today, wouldn't it?

You see, just one or two more houses could make the difference in retiring comfortably or retiring at the poverty level. Surely, after years of working a job just to survive month to month, we all deserve a little more than just eking it out, month to month, when we finally retire.

The solution is quite simple, although it does require some research and a little effort on your part. I'm going to break it right down to the ridiculous just so you really start thinking hard about whether your future will be one of financial insecurity or one of financial independence. You see, after reading this book, if I can provide a solution, the choice really is yours, isn't it?

You and I can do something about it . . . together. I have already obligated myself, my company and my efforts with the National Association of Real Estate Investors to provide a solution to this problem, but there is a breakdown in our solution and this is where you can play a major role. I do want you to know that for your part in helping us remedy this problem, you will be paid a very handsome sum of money, in *cash*. Depending on your particular efforts, that would mean anything from one dollar on up to several hundred thousand dollars. Are you interested in participating if it won't require too much time or any of your own money? Suppose I could even show you how you could help a very worthy cause with your efforts and still make $100,000 doing it. Remember, none of your own money will be involved.

The reason for that is because my company has already spent tens of thousands of dollars to set the foundation and we have provided all of the cash. We simply need your efforts. If you will make a commitment to help me, you will, indirectly, help yourself, your family and your future.

We have spent tens of thousands of dollars researching and developing techniques and methods whereby average people can, with little or no money, purchase rental properties in any city or town in the United States. It doesn't matter whether you are young or old, black or white, are a high school dropout or a commercial airline pilot, there is a potential program for everyone.

Our newsletter is dedicated to bring you new tips throughout the year and step by step guidelines for investing strategies to help a beginner or intermediate investor strive to secure that future for himself and his family, through simple real estate investing.

As you can see, the literature that is available to you as a member and the opportunity to receive our newsletter is not geared just to the person who wants to make a million dollars. We have dedicated our business lives to helping thousands of Americans all over the United States build a better future for themselves.

After you've studied the newsletter, some of our literature and methods, and have become a member of our network, you then may have the use of our network phone service. Here we provide trained investment counselors that will listen to your personal situation and recommend a course of action for you. They have helped many beginners get their first investment for no money down! There is no other support line like this in the United States and we are quite proud of it and invite you to join the team.

Now that I've made my point, I would like to help you actually dig in and apply the ideas we talked about earlier. However, there are some simple questions that you must ask yourself and make a decision on first. These are the same ones I asked myself when I was 20 years old, a high school dropout, working in the slaughterhouse, and had my wife and our first child to support.

1. Do I want a better life for myself and my family?
2. Am I willing to sacrifice a little time after work to do that?
3. Will I apply myself to learn a way to do that?

If your answers to those questions are yes, then you'll want to go on and ask yourself the next set of questions, just as I did.

1. Is there a way to build a fortune if I don't have a lot of money?
2. Is it simple enough so that I don't need extensive education?
3. Is it very risky?
4. Can I start in my spare time, since I presently have a family to support?

After researching the possibilities of investing in real estate, I came to the conclusion that it did fit all of these requirements. I decided to try it, starting with virtually no money at all, while working a full time job.

In just two short years, I was able to gain financial independence and quit my job. At age 27, I became one of America's youngest self-made millionaires, and dedicated my business life to helping other people like me; to learn the same simple methods that helped me turn my life around.

The ingredients that really made me move off center and do something with my life were as follows:

Disgust—I was disgusted with working for someone else, disgusted with just barely paying the bills, disgusted with just stumbling through life and disgusted with not being able to provide better for my family. Yes, disgust could really be the turning point for you, as it was for me.

Decision—You have to make a decision to change. If you want to move off center and change your life, you must make a conscious decision to do so. Believe me, nothing will change your life faster or more positively. You just can't sit on the fence worrying about making the wrong decision. It doesn't really matter what you decide—just decide *something!* We all make bad decisions, but the most important thing that results from them is experience gained to make more intelligent choices in the future.

Action—The most important ingredient of all is action. You can go through all the other items, but to really get going, you have to act. Dare to act and we will arm you with all the support we can to help you, but you must, first, make the decision and ACT!

Remember the story of the man who cried out to the Universe,
"Please give me more time!" and the Universe replied,
"There is no more time—give me more you."

Yours in Success,
Russell A. Whitney